Easy Vegan

Slow Cooker

Cookbook

100 Healthy, Super-Tasty, Fix-And-Forget Vegan
Recipes

SAMANTHA KEATING

ISBN-13: 978-1547291342
ISBN-10: 1547291346

DEDICATION

To all who still give quality time to making home cooking available for their families.

TABLE OF CONTENT

Read Other Books By Samantha Keating:

The Healthy Electric Pressure Cooker Cookbook: 121 Wholesome Recipes For Clean eating, Gluten free, Paleo, Low carb, Vegetarian, Vegan And Mediterranean diet

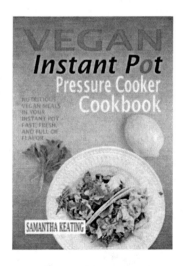

Vegan Instant Pot Pressure Cooker Cookbook: Nutritious Vegan Meals In Your Instant Pot – Fast, Fresh, And Full Of Flavor

Whole Food Challenge: 30 Day Whole Food Diet Meal Plan With
100 Recipes For Healthy Weight Loss (Dairy Free, Gluten Free,
Paleo, Sugar Free And Vegan Recipes)

INTRODUCTION

Your health can greatly improve when you incorporate more plants into your diet. A slow cooker is essential whether you have adopted the full vegan lifestyle or you want to live a healthier life by eating more plant-based foods. Using a slow cooker will make it easier to cook the foods you want without spending unending time in the kitchen fussing over ingredients. Apart from the 100 recipes, this book gives you tips and tricks for preparing easy and delicious meals that will enable you make the most of your slow cooker.

If you are very busy or have a large family to care for, you need a slow cooker to help you manage time in the kitchen. It can work as an oven, a rice cooker or easily become your favorite way of cooking casseroles. Those who work all day can come home to ready to eat meals. This versatile appliance is valuable all year round, in winter to cook hot soups to drive the cold away and in summer to create colorful dishes to impress your friends.

The slow cooker is a wonderful addition to the vegan kitchen. No longer do you have to depend on cans of ingredients that may contain additives that you don't want. You can cook everything from scratch, using fresh ingredients in their natural state. Slow cooking ensures that ingredients are properly blended without overcooking and loss of nutrients.

Slow Cooking Tips And Tricks

Simplicity is one of the main attractions of the slow cooker. Just prepare the ingredients, combine them in the cooker and set the timer. However, there are a few things you need to know if you want great tasting slow-cooked meals every time. Below are some tips to help you create great tasting dishes with your slow cooker.

- Buy The Best Slow Cooker

If you are yet to buy a slow cooker, check online reviews by real users to find out the brands and models that provide the best customer satisfaction. Programmable models will make life much easier for you. They can start cooking at a predetermined time and keep food warm until you are ready to eat. You can also control heat settings at the touch of a button.

- Choose The Right Size

If you don't want to buy different sizes of slow cookers, just choose one that is slightly larger than what your family needs. This will conveniently accommodate more food when you have guests. The 6-quart slow cooker is the most popular.

- Don't Overfill The Cooker

Two-thirds full is the recommendation by most manufacturers. If you fill more than this, you could be exposed to food-safety hazards. Check the owner's manual to be sure.

- Prepare Ahead

Cut vegetables to even sizes as much as possible.

If you want to cook in the morning, prepare the ingredients the night before and refrigerate them in separate containers.

If you're cooking on Low, heat liquids to a simmer before you add them to the cooker.

- Build A Richer Flavor

Browning veggies or herbs like onions, garlic etc in a skillet before adding to the slow cooker will release more flavor. You can skip this step if you are in a hurry, but the food won't taste as good.

- Keep The Lid On

Don't open the lid to look at the meal. When you open the lid, heat escapes and it takes longer to cook. Every peak adds about 15 to 20 minutes to the cooking time. Open the lid only about 30 minutes to the end of the cooking time to check for doneness.

- Don't Use Frozen Ingredients

Thaw all frozen ingredients before adding to the slow cooker.

- Cook At The Right Temperature

Check each recipe for the heat level (HIGH or LOW) and set as specified. If you mistakenly set HIGH for a recipe that should be cooked on LOW, the food with be overcooked.

BREAKFAST AND BREADS

German Style Chocolate Oatmeal

Preparation time: 10 minutes

Cooking time: 6 hours

Servings: 7

Ingredients

2 cups steel cut oats

7 cups water

13.5 ounces coconut milk

¼ cup powdered cocoa, unsweetened

Brown sugar

Shredded coconut, sweetened

Pecans, chopped

Directions:

1. Oil the slow cooker.

2. Pour oats, coconut milk, water and powdered cocoa into a large bowl; stir to mix well.

3. Pour mixture into the slow cooker.

4. Cover, and cook on low for 6 to 8 hours.

5. Top oat in the following order, brown sugar, pecans, shredded coconut to taste. Serve.

Cherry Almond Flavored Oatmeal

Preparation time: 10 minutes

Cooking time: 7 hours

Servings: 7 (3/4 cup)

Ingredients:

3/4 cup tart cherries, dried

1 apple, peeled and grated, ½ cup unsweetened applesauce

2 cups vanilla almond milk, unsweetened

1 to ½ cups water

1 cup steel-cut oats, uncooked

2 tbsp brown sugar

½ tsp almond extract

1 tbsp ground flax seed

¼ tsp salt

Toppings: Maple syrup, toasted sliced almonds or extra almond milk

Directions:

1. Grease the inside of a 3 ½ qt. slow cooker with cooking spray.

2. Pour all the ingredients except optional toppings into the slow cooker, and stir. Cover and cook on low for 7 hours.

3. Scoop oatmeal into bowls, and then add preferred toppings. Serve.

Cooking tips: Refrigerate leftovers until it freezes well. You can double recipe in a 6 qt. slow cooker and increase cooking time 1 hour

To reheat single servings: Pour 1 cup of cooked oatmeal in a microwave proof bowl. Pour in 1/3 cup of almond milk. Microwave on high for 1 minute, and then stir. Cook for additional 1 minute or until it becomes hot.

Creamy Carrot & Zucchini Bread Oatmeal

Preparation time: 10 minutes

Cooking time: 6 to 8 hours

Servings: 2 to 4

Ingredients:

½ cup gluten free steel-cut oats

1½ cups coconut, rice or almond milk

1 small carrot, grated

¼ small zucchini, peeled and grated or more

Pinch of salt

Pinch of ground cloves

Pinch of nutmeg

½ teaspoon cinnamon

2 tablespoons maple syrup or agave nectar

¼ cup chopped pecans

1 teaspoon pure vanilla extract

Directions:

The Night Before: Grease the inside of the slow cooker. Pour all the ingredients except pecans into the slow cooker. Cover and cook on low for 6 to 8 hours.

In The Morning: Stir the oatmeal; taste and adjust the seasonings. Add more milk if required. Top with the chopped pecans.

Apple Cinnamon Crunch Breakfast Pudding

Enjoy a yummy breakfast of pudding with its crunchy cinnamon, nuts or dried fruit topping! Serve with a tall glass of almond milk.

Preparation time: 10 minutes

Cooking time: 4 minutes

Serves: 6

Ingredients:

For Pudding:

1 cup almond milk, unsweetened

2 cups water

2 tbsp maple syrup

½ cup chia seeds

2 tbsp powdered arrowroot

1 tsp ground cinnamon

Pinch of Himalayan rock salt

5 large apples, sliced

Cinnamon Crunch Topping

½ cup almond flour, blanched

¼ cup shredded coconut, unsweetened

¼ cup coconut sugar

1 tsp cinnamon

¼ cup applesauce, unsweetened

1 tsp pure vanilla extract

10

Directions:

1. Pour almond milk, water, chia, maple syrup, cinnamon, arrowroot and salt into a 3 qt. slow cooker. Stir to mix well.

2. Spread sliced apples over the mixture. Do not overlap or combine.

3. In a large bowl, combine the ingredients for cinnamon crumble topping. Spread the mixture over the layered sliced apple with your hands.

4. Cover and cook on high for 2 hours or on low for 4 hours

5. Turn off the heat; unplug the slow cooker and allow to sit while covered for 1 hour.

6. Top pudding with walnuts and raisins. Enjoy!

Cooking tips: To slightly thicken the pudding, corn starch, potato starch or tapioca starch can be used as a substitute for arrowroot. Add preferred protein powder to pudding to increase the protein content, if desired.

Banana 'N' Coconut Milk Oatmeal

Preparation time: 10 minutes

Cooking time: 7 hours

Servings: 7 (3/4 cup)

Ingredients:

2 medium-size ripe bananas, sliced (or 2 cups of sliced ripe bananas)

1 cup steel cut oats

14 ounces light coconut milk

1 tbsp ground flax seed

½ tsp vanilla

½ tsp cinnamon

¼ tsp nutmeg

2 tbsp brown sugar

¼ tsp kosher salt

Optional toppings: additional sliced bananas, macadamia nuts or walnuts, toasted coconut, maple syrup, additional brown sugar or additional coconut milk

Directions:

1. Grease the inside of a 3 ½ qt. slow cooker with cooking spray.

2. Pour all the ingredients except optional toppings into the slow cooker, and stir. Cover and cook on low for 7 hours.

3. Scoop oatmeal into bowls, and then add preferred toppings. Serve.

Cooking tips: Refrigerate leftovers until it freezes well. You can double recipe in a 6 qt. slow cooker and increase cooking time to 1 hour.

To reheat single servings: Pour 1 cup of cooked oatmeal in a microwave proof bowl. Pour in 1/3 cup of almond milk. Microwave on high for 1 minute, and then stir. Cook for additional 1 minute or until it becomes hot.

Creamy Vanilla Flavored Coconut Steel Cut Oats

Preparation time: 10 minutes

Cooking time: 8 hours

Servings: 6 to 8

Ingredients:

2 cups steel cut oatmeal

1 can full fat coconut milk

8 cups water

1 tsp vanilla

2 tbsp coconut sugar or organic cane sugar (optional)

Directions:

1. Pour all the ingredients into a slow cooker. Cover and cook on low for 8 hours or until it becomes creamy.

2. Serve oatmeal with coconut flakes, dried fruit, nut butter, pumpkin seeds, chia seeds, raisins, etc.

Slow Cooked Quinoa Breakfast

Preparation time: 5 minutes

Cooking time: High: 2 to 3 hours, Low: 8 hours

Servings: 5

Ingredients:

1 cup quinoa

3 cups almond milk

4 medjool dates, chopped

¼ cup pepitas

1 apple, peeled and diced

2 teaspoons cinnamon

¼ teaspoon nutmeg

1 teaspoon vanilla extract

¼ teaspoon salt

Directions:

1. Pour all the ingredients into the slow cooker.

2. Cover and cook on high for 2 hours or until all the liquid is absorbed.

Cooking tips: Set slow cooker on low before going to bed to cook quinoa overnight. It should be ready by morning. Cook on low for 8 hours. Place in a refrigerator for up to 1 week.

Apple Granola Breakfast

Preparation time: 10 minutes

Cooking time: High: 2-3 hours; Low: 7-9 hours

Servings: 5

Ingredients:

4 apples, sliced and peeled if desired

2 cups gluten-free granola

¼ cup maple syrup

2 tablespoons melted coconut oil

1 teaspoon cinnamon

Directions:

1. Coat the slow cooker with a cooking spray. Place sliced apples in the slow cooker.

2. Combine granola, applesauce, maple syrup, cinnamon and coconut oil in a medium-size mixing bowl. Stir until properly mixed.

3. Pour the granola mixture over the slices apples.

4. Cover and cook on high for 2 to 3 hours or on low for 7 to 9 hours or overnight.

Breakfast Sorghum - Pumpkin Pie

Enjoy your breakfast made with sorghum, a gluten-free whole grain with an increased level of antioxidants.

Preparation time: 10 minutes

Cooking time: 8 hours

Servings: 4

Ingredients:

1 cup gluten-free sorghum, rinsed

1 cup almond milk, unsweetened

¾ cup pumpkin purée (not pumpkin pie filling)

2 tablespoon pure maple syrup

1 tablespoon pumpkin pie spice

1 teaspoon pure vanilla extract

Directions:

1. Combine all the ingredients and 2 cups of water in a 3 to 4 qt. slow cooker. Stir to mix properly.

2. Cover and cook on low for 8 hours or until sorghum is soft and the liquid is absorbed.

Cooking tips: Store meal in a covered container and stored in a refrigerator. Individual servings can be spooned out and reheated.

To reheat: Scoop meal into a small saucepan. Add water or a splash of almond milk, and then cook over medium heat or until properly heated.

Breakfast Pumpkin Oatmeal Bars

Preparation time: 10 minutes

Cooking time: 2 hours

Servings: 16

Ingredients:

1 ¾ cup canned pumpkin puree

2/3 cup coconut sugar

3 tablespoons maple syrup

1 teaspoon raw apple cider vinegar

1 cup old fashioned oats, rolled

1 cup oat flour

1 tablespoon pumpkin pie spice

½ tablespoon cinnamon

1 teaspoon baking soda

¼ teaspoon salt

1/3 cups toasted pecans, coarsely chopped, divided

Directions:

1. Place a 7 qt. slow cooker on a large slow cooker liner or parchment paper. Trace the bottom of the slow cooker and cut out the traced part leaving some overhang.

2. Coat the bottom the slow cooker with cooking spray. Press the slow cooker liner or parchment paper into the bottom; overhang will be used as handles.

3. Combine pumpkin, maple syrup, coconut sugar and apple cider vinegar in a large bowl, and then stir.

4. Pour in the oats, cinnamon, oat flour, baking soda, pumpkin pie spice, ¼ cup of the pecans and salt. Stir until properly mixed and thick dough is formed.

5. Scoop the mixture into the slow cooker and then spread it out evenly. Top with the remaining pecans.

6. Cover and cook on low for 1 ½ to 2 hours or until the top looks cooked. Take note not to over-bake. Turn off the slow cooker and let the bars sit for 1 hour to cool.

7. Lift the bar out of the pan gently, and then transfer to a wire rack to cool.

8. Slice into bars and enjoy!

Yummy Chocolate Walnut Oatmeal

Preparation time: 10 minutes

Cooking time: 7 to 9 hours

Servings: 2 to 3

Ingredients:

½ cup steel-cut oats

2 cups coconut milk, unsweetened

1 tsp vanilla extract

1 - 2 tbsp sweetener

1 tbsp vegan chocolate chips, (whole or chopped)

2 tbsp walnuts, chopped

Directions:

1. The night before: Grease the slow cooker with cooking spray. Pour all the ingredients except the chocolate chips and walnuts into the slow cooker.

2. Cover and cook on low for 7 to 9 hour over night.

3. In the morning: Stir the oatmeal together to get a uniform consistency. Top with walnuts and chopped chocolate chips.

APPETIZERS AND SNACKS

Slow Cooked Apple Crisp

Preparation time: 15 minutes

Cooking time: 4 hours

Servings: 8

Ingredients:

6 cups chopped apples

¾ cup packed brown sugar

¼ cup cane sugar

¾ cup all-purpose flour

1 tablespoon corn starch

2 tablespoons apple pie spice

1 tablespoon apple butter

4 ½ tablespoons applesauce

¼ cup chopped walnuts

Dash of salt

2 tablespoons lemon juice

For garnishing: Vegan ice cream

Directions:

1. Pour chopped apples into the slow cooker. Add lemon juice and apple butter, and then stir properly to coat the apples.

2. Combine corn starch, ¼ cup of cane sugar and 1 tbsp of apple pie spice in a bowl. Stir until properly mixed. Pour mixture over apple and top with walnuts, and then mix well.

3. Combine flour, the remaining apple pie spice, brown sugar and salt in another bowl. Use a pastry cutter to cut apple butter into the mixture. Pour mixture into the slow cooker and stir until crumbly like sand. Sprinkle vegan ice cream over the apple mixture until completely covered.

4. Cover and cook on low for 4 hours, or until the apples are soft and tender. If you choose to make this over night, make sure your slow cooker turns off when it's done so the crisp doesn't burn.

Healthy Cereal Mix

Preparation time: 10 minutes

Cooking time: 1 hour 50 minutes

Servings: 16 cups

Ingredients:

3 cups corn cereal

3 cups rice cereal

3 cups wheat cereal

3 cups fruit cereal

3 cups homemade pretzel sticks

1 can mixed nuts

1 cup vegetable oil

2 tbsp Worcestershire sauce

1 ½ tsp seasoned salt

¾ tsp powdered garlic

Directions:

1. Combine the wheat cereal, rice cereal, corn cereal, fruit cereal, mixed nuts and pretzel sticks in a 6-qt. or larger slow cooker.

2. In a bowl, whisk together vegetable oil, powdered garlic, Worcestershire sauce and seasoned salt, and then pour over the cereal mixture. Stir until properly mixed.

3. Cook mixture uncovered on high for 1 ½ hours and stirring often.

4. Reduce the slow cooker to low and cook for another 20 minutes and stirring frequently.

5. Spread cooked mixture on a cookie sheet to cool.

Tasty And Spicy Mushroom

Preparation time: 10 minutes

Cooking time: 2 to 6 hours

Servings: 8

Ingredients:

½ cup hoisin sauce

¼ cup water

2 tbsp minced garlic

½ to ¾ tsp crushed red pepper

24 oz. clean fresh mushrooms

Directions:

1. Pour hoisin sauce, powdered garlic, water and red pepper into a 3 ½ to 4-qt. slow cooker. Stir until properly mixed.

2. Pour in the mushrooms and toss to coat.

3. Cover and cook on high for 2 to 3 hours or on low for 5 to 6 hours.

4. Serve spicy mushrooms with toothpicks.

Cajun Boiled Peanuts

Preparation time: 10 minutes

Cooking time: 12 to 24 hours

Servings: 5

Ingredients:

1 lb raw peanuts, still in the shell

1 tbsp powdered garlic

½ cup salt

2 tbsp Cajun seasoning

2 tbsp red pepper flakes

8 cups water

Directions:

1. Pour peanuts into a slow cooker. Add water.

2. Pour powdered garlic, Cajun seasoning, salt and pepper over the peanuts. Stir until everything mixes together.

3. Cover and cook on low for 12 to 24 hours. The longer the peanuts cook, the stronger the flavor will become.

4. Add additional water if needed so peanuts are completely covered.

5. Use a slotted spoon to scoop the peanuts out and serve in a bowl.

Pumpkin Spice Cinnamon Buns

Preparation time: 20 minutes

Cooking time: 2 hours

Servings: 12 to 14 rolls

Ingredients:

3 cups all purpose flour

1/4 cup sugar

1 package active dry yeast

½ cup vanilla almond milk

¼ cup water

¾ cup pureed pumpkin

½ cup canola oil

1 Flaxseed egg (Add 1 tbsp flaxseed to 1 ½ tbsp warm water, and then let it sit for 5 minutes)

For Filling:

1/3 cup apple butter

1/3 cup brown sugar

2 teaspoons ground cinnamon

2 teaspoons nutmeg

1 teaspoon ginger

1 teaspoon ground gloves

For Icing:

4 ounces soft vegan cream cheese

1 cup powdered sugar

½ stick vegan butter, soft

½ teaspoon vanilla extract

½ teaspoon lemon juice

Directions:

1. Combine flour, yeast and sugar in a large bowl. Fold pumpkin, almond milk, flaxseed egg, water and oil into dry ingredients. Mold into a ball and set aside for 30 to 45 minutes in a bowl, covered with a towel.

2. Once the dough is settled, place on a lightly floured surface and mold into a rectangle.

3. Combine the filling ingredients in a bowl.

4. Baste the rolled rectangle dough with the sugary, pumpkin spice mixture. Roll the dough long side to long side. Next, pinch both ends and then cut into 12 to 14 slices.

5. Place sliced dough in a coated slow cooker. Cover and cook on high for 60 to 90 minutes. Dip a toothpick into rolls to determine doneness. If it comes out clean, then it's ready!

6. Combine the icing ingredients and pour over hot rolls to get a gooey and really moist cinnamon bun. If desired, top with pecan pieces.

Spiced Nuts

Preparation time: 10 minutes

Cooking time: 2 ½ hours

Servings: 7

Ingredients:

1 lb. pecans, walnuts, cashew or preferred nuts

½ cup olive oil

½ cup powdered sugar

¼ teaspoon ground nutmeg

1/8 teaspoon ground cloves

1 ½ teaspoons ground cinnamon

¼ teaspoon ground ginger

½ teaspoon ground cardamom

Directions:

1. Preheat the slow cooker on high for 15 minutes. Add the olive oil and nuts, and then stir until properly mixed. Pour in the powdered sugar, stirring to coat evenly.

2. Cover and cook on high for 15 minutes. Reduce heat to low, uncover and cook for 2 hours, stirring occasionally until the nuts are well coated and crisp.

3. Transfer crispy nuts to a bowl.

4. Combine the spices in a small bowl and then sift mixture over the nuts. Stir together to coat evenly. Let it cool before serving.

Spiced Chickpeas And Potatoes

This recipe combines a variety of spices including garam masala. Hmmm yummy!

Preparation time: 15 minutes

Cooking time: 4 to 9 hours

Servings: 6

Ingredients:

1 tbsp olive oil

1 large white or yellow onion, diced about ¼ inch (or 1 ½ cups)

3 garlic cloves, finely minced

2 tsp dried ground coriander

1 tbsp ground cumin

1 tsp garam masala

½ tsp ground ginger

½ tsp ground turmeric

¼ tsp red pepper flakes

Pinch of cayenne pepper

1 tsp salt

1/8 tsp black pepper

15 oz. diced tomatoes, with juice

3 tbsp tomato paste

1 cup vegetable stock

2 (15 oz.) cans chickpeas, drained, rinsed and dried with a paper towel

1 lb. red potatoes, peeled and diced about ½-inch thick

2 tsp fresh lime juice

2 cups roughly chopped kale leaves, ribs removed

¼ cup chopped cilantro leaves

Directions:

1. Pour olive oil into a large sauté pan and heat over medium heat. Add the chopped onion and cook, stir until it becomes translucent. Add garlic, garam masala, coriander, turmeric, cumin, ginger, cayenne pepper, red pepper flakes, black pepper and salt. Cook over low heat for 1 minute, stirring frequently.

2. Pour in the diced tomatoes with juice, vegetable stock and tomato paste.

3. Pour chickpeas and diced potatoes into a 4-qt. slow cooker. Pour the tomato and onion mixture over it and gently stir to combine.

4. Cover and cook on low for 8 to 9 hours or on high for 4 to 5 hours or until potatoes are tender.

5. Pour in the lime juice, kale leaves and chopped cilantro. Stir gently until properly mixed. Let mixture cool for 5 minutes to wilt the kale leaves. Serve with basmati rice.

Easy Corn Dip

Preparation time: 10 minutes

Cooking time: 3 hours

Servings: 4

Ingredients:

4 oz. green chilies

16 oz. vegan cream cheese

1 cup vegan sour cream

1 jalapeno

2 pounds frozen corn

Directions:

1. Pour 2 lbs. of corn into a slow cooker. Cook on low heat.

2. Cut vegan cheese cream into cubes and pour into the slow cooker. Add 1 cup of vegan sour cream and green chilies.

3. Chop the jalapeno (remove the seed before dicing if you don't like a lot of spice). You can use half a jalapeno. Pour into the slow cooker.

4. Cover and cook on low for 3 hours.

5. Serve meal with Fritos or tortilla chips.

Sweet Jalapeno Corn Dip

Preparation time: 5 minutes

Cooking time: 3 hours

Servings: 4

Ingredients:

16 ounces frozen sweet corn

1 diced jalapeno, seeds and ribs removed (or leave seeds in if you want it hot)

8 ounces chive and vegan onion flavored cream cheese

½ cup shredded vegan parmesan cheese

½ cup shredded vegan Gouda cheese

½ tsp powdered garlic

Directions:

1. Pour all the ingredients in a slow cooker.

2. Cover and cook on low for 2 to 3 hours or until melted

Tasty Mushrooms

Preparation time: 15 minutes

Cooking time: 2 hours, 30 minutes

Servings: 4

Ingredients:

1 lb. medium to large size white button mushrooms

1 to 4 cups finely chopped fresh flat leaf parsley

2 tbsp extra virgin olive oil

3 garlic cloves, finely chopped

1 tsp kosher salt

¼ tsp black ground pepper

Directions:

1. Trim off mushroom ends leaving a little bit of the stem. Do not pop out like you would with stuffed mushrooms.

2. Clean mushrooms with a damp cloth. Do not float them in water when cleaning because mushrooms absorb water.

3. Cut mushrooms into quarters or decent sizes.

4. Pour all the remaining ingredients into the slow cooker and stir to mix well.

5. Cover and cook on high 2 to 3 hours.

6. Place tasty mushrooms in a bowl and serve with toothpicks as an appetizer.

Tasty Garlic Lime Hummus

Preparation time: 5 minutes

Cooking time: 8 hours

Servings: 8

Ingredients:

½ lb. chick peas, dried, picked over, soaked, and drained

¼ cup tahini

1 tbsp chopped garlic

2 tbsp olive oil

2-4 tbsp fresh lime juice

Directions:

1. Pour chick peas in the slow cooker. Cover and cook on low for 8 to 10 hours or until it becomes very tender. Drain the beans.

2. Pour cooked beans, garlic, tahini, and olive oil into the bowl of a food processor fitted with a metal blade, and then process until very smooth.

3. Pour in enough lime juice and process until desired consistency is achieved.

4. Add salt to taste. Allow to sit and chill until it's ready to serve.

5. Hummus can be refrigerated.

SOUPS

Chard, Lentil & Potato Soup

Prepare a delicious tasty vegan soup with chard, lentil and potato.

Preparation time: 20 minutes

Cooking time: 8 hours

Servings: 6

Ingredients:

1 tablespoon olive oil

1 large size yellow onion, chopped

1 celery stalk, sliced

1 large carrot, sliced

2 garlic cloves, minced

1 large bunch Swiss chard, stem sliced and leaves torn into bite-sized pieces

1 cup brown lentils, dried, picked over and rinsed

4 medium Yukon Gold potatoes, diced into 1-inch pieces

6 cups vegetable broth

1 tablespoon tamari

Pepper and kosher salt to taste

Directions:

1. Pour oil into a large skillet and heat over medium heat. Pour in the onion, carrot, celery, Swiss chard stems and garlic.

2. Cover the skillet and cook for 8 to 10 minutes or until softened, stirring occasionally.

3. Pour the cooked vegetable mixture, potatoes, lentils, tamari and broth into a 4 to 6-qt. slow cooker. Stir to mix well.

4. Cover and cook on low for 8 hours.

5. Before the soup is ready, pour water in a large pot and bring to a boil. Place reserved chard leaves in the boiling water and cook for 5 minutes or until it becomes tender.

6. Drain well and stir cooked chard into soup. Add pepper and salt to taste.

Creamy Parsnip And Butternut Squash Soup

Preparation time: 10 minutes

Cooking time: 6 hours

Servings: 4 to 6

Ingredients:

1 large size yellow onion, finely chopped

2 parsnips, peeled and chopped

1 small peeled and seeded butternut squash, chopped into small squares (about 5 cups)

1 peeled fuji apple, chopped

2 cups vegetable broth

½ tsp ground coriander

½ tsp ground cumin

¼ tsp dried thyme

1/8 tsp ground sage

½ tsp kosher salt

For serving: Coconut cream

Directions:

1. Pour all the ingredients into a slow cooker.

2. Cover and cook on low for 6 hours.

3. Once the vegetables are cooked, pour the soup in batches into a blender and process until smooth.

4. Serve soup with coconut cream and crusty bread.

Leek And Potato Soup

Preparation time: 15 minutes

Cooking time: 4 hours

Servings: 6

Ingredients:

2 large size leeks, washed, cut off ends and sliced thinly

4 large size russet potatoes, peeled and quartered

3 carrots, washed and finely chopped

2 celery stalks, finely chopped

2 cloves garlic, minced

Pepper and kosher salt to taste

4 to 6 cups vegetable broth (or enough to cover the veggies)

For garnishing: Croutons, fresh parsley (optional)

Directions:

1. Pour the leeks, carrots, potatoes, garlic and celery in a slow cooker. Add pepper and salt to taste. Pour in the vegetable broth, to cover up the veggies.

2. Cover and cook on low for 6 hours or on high for 4 hours.

3. Blend soup smooth with an immersion blender, or pour soup in batches into a food processor. Blend until smooth. Adjust pepper and salt to taste.

4. Scoop soup into serving bowls. Add the croutons and parsley. Serve.

Vegan Miso Split Pea Soup

Savor the simmering aroma of miso split pea soup in your slow cooker!

Preparation time: 10 minutes

Cooking time: 6 hours

Servings: 4

Ingredients:

5 cups vegetable broth

4 to 5 cups water (or more)

4 cups split peas, dried and rinsed

1 cup finely chopped carrots

2 garlic cloves, minced

1 large onion, finely chopped

3 to 4 tbsp white miso paste

3 tbsp coconut oil

Pepper and salt to taste

Directions:

1. Chop the onion, garlic and carrots, and then pour into a slow cooker. Pour in the coconut oil and miso paste; stir until properly mixed and coated.

2. Pour all the remaining ingredients into the slow cooker, pour liquid on last.

3. Cover and cook high for 4 to 6 hours, mixing occasionally. Add pepper and salt to taste.

4. Allow to cool before serving.

Collard And Bean Delicata Squash Soup

Preparation time: 10 minutes

Cooking time: 5 hours

Servings: 4

Ingredients:

5 cups of filtered water or vegetable broth

2 delicata squashes, peeled, seeds removed, chopped

2 cups kidney beans, cooked

3 to 4 collard green leaves, ribs removed and finely chopped

1 fennel bulb, chopped (or 5 celery stalks)

1 onion, diced

1 large shallot, chopped

3 garlic cloves, minced

1 tbsp coconut oil or extra virgin olive

5 fresh sage leaves, chopped

½ to 1 tsp turmeric

½ tsp paprika

1 tsp of dried parsley or a handful of fresh, chopped

Generous pinch of ground celery seed and dried thyme

Coarse ground pepper and sea salt, to taste

Directions:

1. Pour all the ingredients except beans and collards into the slow cooker. Cover and cook on low for 4 hours or until the veggies are soft and tender.

2. Add the beans and collards, and then cook for 1 hour. The soup is ready when the collards are properly cooked or turns bright green and wilted. Enjoy!

Italian Style Vegan Bean Soup

Preparation time: 10 minutes

Cooking time: 5 hours

Servings: 4

Ingredients:

1 lb. dried Great Northern Beans

2 ribs of celery, finely chopped

1 small onion, chopped

3 carrots, peeled and chopped

1 tablespoon fennel seeds

2 teaspoons dried oregano leaves

2 teaspoons powdered garlic

¼ teaspoon red pepper flakes (optional)

Pepper and salt to taste

6 tablespoons grated vegan parmesan cheese (optional)

Directions:

1. Pour beans, onion, celery, carrots, oregano, fennel seeds, powdered garlic, red pepper flakes and 5 cups of cold water into a 3 qt. slow cooker.

2. Cover and cook on high for 5 hours or until beans are tender.

3. You may drain to remove beans cooking liquid which sometimes causes gas. Drained or not, you need to add more liquid. Add 2 to 4 cups of water until the desired thickness consistency is achieved.

4. Stir soup and then add pepper and salt to taste.

5. Scoop soup into serving bowls. Sprinkle 1 tbsp of vegan parmesan cheese over each serving if desired.

African Style Vegan Soup

Preparation time: 10 minutes

Cooking time: 4 to 8 hours

Servings: 6 to 8

Ingredients:

1 medium size yellow onion, finely chopped

¼ cup sliced green onion

2 red bell peppers, seeds removed and diced into ½ inch pieces

1 tablespoon minced garlic

28 ounces diced tomatoes with juice

8 cups vegetable stock

1 teaspoon ground cumin

1 tablespoon Ancho powdered chili

1 teaspoon New Mexico powdered chili

1 teaspoon Aleppo pepper

½ cup brown lentils, uncooked

¼ cup brown rice, uncooked

1 cup peanut butter or natural peanut butter, unsweetened

Directions:

1. Chop onions, bell peppers, green onion and garlic and pour into the slow cooker.

2. Pour in the tomatoes with juice, vegetable broth, Aleppo pepper, ground cumin, Ancho powdered chili, lentil, New Mexico powdered chili and brown rice.

3. Cover and cook on low for 8 hours or on high for 4 hours. Stir once or twice while cooking but not essential.

4. After the cooking time, reduce heat to low and add the peanut butter while stirring. Cook on low for another 1 hour or on high for 30 minutes. Serve hot.

Note: Store soup in a refrigerator. This soup is great to have in hand during spring days that feel like winter.

Black Bean And Brown Rice Soup

Prepare the perfect and hearty weeknight dinner with black beans and brown rice. This soup is thick and deliciously tasty.

Preparation time: 20 minutes

Cooking time: 8 hours

Servings: 6

Ingredients:

60 oz. black beans, drained but not rinsed (reserve 15 oz. for later use)

1 tbsp olive oil

1 cup diced yellow onion (about ½ of a medium onion)

2 medium size carrots, diced (1 cup diced carrot)

¼ cup diced jalapeno pepper (or 1 medium size deseeded jalapeno pepper, finely diced)

2 to 3 medium size garlic cloves, minced (or 1 tbsp minced garlic)

1 tsp powdered chili

1 tsp cumin

1 tsp dried oregano

½ tsp kosher salt (or more to taste)

¼ tsp freshly ground black pepper

4 cups vegetable broth

2 tbsp tomato paste

10 dashes Tabasco sauce, or to taste

2 cups brown rice, cooked

Fresh lime wedges

Optional toppings: Diced tomatoes, vegan sour cream, diced scallions, cilantro leaves and avocado

Directions:

1. Pour 45 oz. of black beans into a 3 qt. or larger slow cooker.

2. Heat up olive oil in a large sauté pan over medium heat. Pour in carrots and onions; sauté for 5 minutes or until onion is soft and translucent.

3. Pour in the jalapeno pepper, powdered chili, garlic, oregano, cumin, pepper and salt, and then sauté while stirring for additional minute. Add tomato paste, Tabasco sauce and vegetable broth; stir until the tomato paste is completely dissolved.

4. Pour sautéed mixture over the beans in the slow cooker.

5. Cover and cook on low 6 to 8 hours.

6. Uncover and allow to cool for a while until it's safe to handle. Blend soup using an immersion blender or pour soup in batches into a food processor or blender; process into smooth puree.

7. Pour the smooth soup into the slow cooker, and then add the reserved 15 oz. of beans and rice.

8. Cover and cook on medium for 30 minutes. Adjust pepper and salt to taste. Add more Tabasco if desired.

9. Ladle soup into serving bowls. Squeeze a lime wedge over the top of each serving. Add preferred toppings. Serve.

Note: Store soup in an airtight container and place in a refrigerator for 3 to 4 days. Add vegetable broth to thin leftover soup before serving because it can thicken over time.

Veggie Mixed Bean Soup

Preparation time: 10 minutes

Cooking time: 4 to 8 hours

Servings: 6

Ingredients:

1½ cups bean and grain soup mix

1 large onion, finely chopped

4 medium carrots, scrubbed and diced

4 large garlic cloves, minced

7 cups vegetable stock

Black pepper and salt

1 tbsp minced fresh thyme

Optional toppings: Fresh lemon wedges

Directions:

1. The night before: Soak soup mix in a bowl of cold water.

2. The next morning: Rinse and drain the soup mix.

3. Pour all the ingredients except lemon wedges and thyme into the slow cooker, and then stir. Adjust black pepper and salt to taste.

4. Cover and cook on low 6 to 8 hours, make sure to check after 6 hours of cooking or cook on high for 4 to 5 hours. Do not open the slow cooker until after 4 hours of cooking.

5. Once it's ready, add thyme and stir. Taste and adjust pepper and salt to taste.

6. If desired, squeeze fresh lemon wedges over the top. Serve.

Tomato Basil Soup

Preparation time: 15 minutes

Cooking time: 4 hours

Servings: 3 to 4

Ingredients:

2 tbsp olive oil

1 cup carrot, peeled and finely chopped

1 yellow onion, diced

1 cup celery, finely chopped

6 garlic cloves, minced

½ tsp ground sage

¼ tsp dried oregano

¼ tsp dried thyme

½ tsp kosher salt

42 oz. diced tomatoes with juice

2 cups vegetable broth

2 cups almond milk, unsweetened

1/3 cup chopped fresh basil leaves or 3 tbsp basil paste

Directions:

1. Pour oil into a skillet and heat over medium heat. Add onion, celery and carrots, and then sauté while stirring often for 15 minutes or until veggies are tender.

2. Add garlic, oregano, sage, thyme, and salt, and then sauté for another 2 minutes.

3. Pour sautéed veggies into the slow cooker. Add the remaining ingredients and cook on low for 4 hours.

4. Pour tomato basil soup in batches into a blender and process until smooth.

5. Serve soup with delicious sandwich or rustic, crusty bread.

STEWS, CHILIES AND CURRIES

Vegan Corn 'N' Red Pepper Chowder

This chowder version is lighter, sweet, smoky and filled with flavor. Savor its aroma while it simmers in the slow cooker. This is the perfect meal for a weeknight dinner.

Preparation time: 30 minutes

Cooking time: 8 hours

Servings: 4 to 6

Ingredients:

2 tbsp olive oil

2 cups diced yellow onion (or 1 medium yellow onion, diced)

1 medium size red bell pepper, seeded and chopped

3 cups diced Yukon Gold potatoes (or 3 medium (1 lb) Yukon Gold potatoes, diced)

4 cups sweet corn kernels, frozen or fresh and divided (approx. 4 ears of corn)

4 cups vegetable broth

1 tsp ground cumin

½ tsp smoked paprika

1/8 tsp cayenne pepper

1 tsp kosher salt

1 cup almond milk

Freshly ground black pepper and salt to taste

For garnishing: Chopped red bell pepper, sliced scallions and corn kernels

Directions:

1. Pour olive oil into a medium sauté pan and heat over medium heat. Add onion and cook while stirring often for 5 minutes or until it becomes translucent and soft.

2. Pour sautéed onion into the slow cooker. Add red bell pepper, vegetable broth, potatoes, cumin, 1 cup corn, smoked paprika, pepper, and salt.

3. Cover and cook on high for 4 to 6 hours or on low for 8 to 10 hours or until the potatoes are soft.

4. Turn off the slow cooker and uncover. Allow the soup to cool slightly. Blend soup until smooth with an immersion blender or pour soup in batches into a blender and process until smooth.

5. Pour smooth soup into the slow cooker and turn it on. Stir in the remaining 3 cups of corn and almond milk.

6. Cover and cook on low for 20 to 30 minutes or until the soup is properly heated through. Add pepper and salt to taste.

7. Top soup with extra corn, pepper and scallions. Serve.

Vegetarian Lentil Chili

Enjoy your slow cooker lentil chili with your favorite chili toppings. This chili is vegan and gluten-free, loved by vegetarians and meat lovers alike.

Preparation time: 10 minutes

Cooking time: 4 to 6 hours

Servings: 8 to 10

Ingredients:

1 medium-size onion, chopped

3 garlic cloves, minced

1 jalapeño, seeds removed and diced

1 red pepper, finely chopped

1 yellow pepper, diced

1 large peeled carrot, chopped

2 ½ cups vegetable broth

30 ounces tomato sauce

30 ounces diced tomatoes

16 oz. (1 bag) brown lentils, rinsed

2 (15 oz) cans small red beans, rinsed and drained

3 tbsp powdered chili

1 tbsp cumin

Black pepper and salt to taste

Directions:

1. Pour all the ingredients into a 6 qt. slow cooker. Stir until completely mixed.

2. Cover and cook on low for 6 hours or on high for 4 hours.

3. Top with favorite chili toppings. Serve when warm.

Cooking tips: Store in a refrigerator. There have been some complaints about lentils not cooking in a slow cooker. The lentils cooked well in this recipe but to be safe, you may prefer to cook them before adding them to the slow cooker.

Chipotle Black Bean Stew

Preparation time: 10 minutes

Cooking time: 4 to 6 hours

Servings: 6 to 8

Ingredients:

1 to 2 dried chipotle peppers

1 lb. of dried organic black beans, picked over, rinsed and soaked overnight

¾ cup uncooked quinoa, picked over and rinsed

28 oz. (1 can) organic diced tomatoes

1 red onion, chopped

3 garlic cloves, minced

1 green bell pepper, diced

1 red bell pepper, finely chopped

1 dried cinnamon stick

2 tsp powdered chili

1 tsp powdered coriander

¼ cup fresh cilantro

7 cups water

Pepper and sea salt to taste

For topping: cilantro, lime wedges, green onions, thinly sliced and avocado

Directions:

1. Pour all the ingredients except salt, into the slow-cooker, stir to mix well. You many sauté the onion, bell pepper and garlic first if preferred.

2. Cover and cook on low for 8 to 10 hours or on high for 4 to 6 hours, or until black beans are soft (cooking time depends on the freshness of beans and the strength of your slow cooker). Add salt at the very end, as it will affect how the beans cook, if you add it at the beginning.

3. Remove the chipotles (if you don't want your stew spicy) and the cinnamon stick before serving.

4. Spoon stew into serving bowls. Top with fresh cilantro, a squeeze of fresh lemon juice, green onions, diced avocado, tortilla chips, vegan sour cream, hot sauce, etc.

Cooker Creamy Lentil Cauliflower Stew

Preparation time: 30 minutes

Cooking time: 8 hours

Servings: 8 to 10

Ingredients:

16 ounces dried lentils

1 tablespoon olive oil

2 cups chopped onion (or 1 large onion, chopped)

2 garlic cloves, finely chopped

1 lb. cauliflower, diced into very small florets

2 leeks, white and green parts only, halved, washed carefully, and chopped

2 large peeled carrots, chopped

3 celery stalks, finely chopped

2 bay leaves

1 tablespoon chopped fresh thyme (or 1 tsp dried thyme)

Kosher salt to taste

1 teaspoon cumin

¼ to ½ teaspoon cayenne

¼ teaspoon black pepper

8 cups vegetable broth

32 oz. (1 large can) diced tomatoes with juice

2 cups chopped Swiss chard or kale

Optional toppings: Coconut cream, vegan sour cream, feta, grated vegan Parmesan

Directions:

1. Arrange the lentils, discard stones or dirt. Wash the lentils in a wire mesh strainer.

2. Pour oil into a skillet and heat over medium heat. Sauté the onion for 4 minutes or until it becomes soft. Pour in the chopped garlic and sauté for another minute.

3. Pour sautéed onions and garlic mixture into the slow cooker and then add the remaining ingredients except the toppings.

4. Cover and cook on high for 6 hours or on low for 8 hours or until the lentils are tender.

5. Top with preferred toppings and serve hot.

Vegan Chili With Farro

Preparation time: 10 minutes

Cooking time: 8 hours

Servings: 6 to 8

Ingredients:

For the chili:

1 red onion, finely chopped

1 green pepper, diced

1 orange pepper, chopped

8 oz. (1 pkg.) baby bella mushrooms, sliced

14 oz. (2 cans) diced fire-roasted tomatoes

15 oz. (1 can) black beans, drained and rinsed

15 oz. (1 can) pinto beans, drained and rinsed

15 oz. (1 can) kidney beans, drained and rinsed

3 cups vegetable broth

1 cup farro, rinsed and drained

1 to 3 chipotle peppers in adobo sauce, minced

1 ½ tbsp powdered chili

2 tsp cumin

2 tsp powdered garlic

1 tsp salt

Optional toppings: Coconut cream, vegan sour cream, sliced green onions, vegan shredded cheddar cheese, chopped cilantro, tortilla chips, sliced avocado

Directions:

1. Pour all the ingredients for the chili into a 6-qt. slow cooker. Stir until well mixed.

2. Cover the slow cooker and cook on low for 6 to 8 hours.

3. When done, the chili should have slightly thickened up and the veggies tender. Add pepper and salt to taste, if needed. Top with desired toppings. Serve.

Cooking tips: 1 chipotle pepper will give you a really mild spice while 3 full ones will give it a kick; this depends on your taste. Add a splash of vegetable broth to thickened chili leftover when reheating. This will make it thin and loosen it up.

Creamy Veggie Red Thai Curry

This red Thai curry is packed with veggies and flavored with coconut cream or milk.

Preparation time: 15 minutes

Cooking time: 4 hours, 30 minutes

Servings: 6 to 8

Ingredients:

½ head cauliflower, chopped into florets

2 medium-size peeled sweet potatoes cut into cubes

1 small onion, diced

14 oz. (1 can) light coconut milk (or coconut cream)

3 tablespoons tamari

1 to 2 teaspoons Sriracha sauce (or to desired spice)

½ teaspoon salt (to taste)

3 tablespoons red curry paste

1 tablespoon brown sugar

8 oz. white mushrooms, quartered

1 cup fresh green peas (or frozen)

Brown rice, cooked

For garnishing:

½ cup toasted cashews

¼ cup chopped fresh cilantro

Fresh basil leaves

Directions:

1. Wash and chop the cauliflower, onion and sweet potatoes. Pour them into the slow cooker.

2. Meanwhile, chop the cilantro and mushrooms, and then set them aside. Toast the cashews for 5 to 7 minutes in a preheated oven of 350°F if using raw ones, and then set aside.

3. Combine coconut milk, tamari, red curry paste, sriracha sauce, brown sugar and salt in a small bowl. Add 1 tsp of sriracha sauce if you have a low tolerance for spicy food; add more if you want more heat.

4. Pour the mixture over the veggies in the slow cooker, and then stir until the vegetables are completely coated.

5. Cover and cook on low for 4 hours.

6. Add the peas and mushrooms, and cook for 30 minutes.

7. At this time, start cooking the rice. Add salt to taste.

8. Serve curry over steamy rice and top with the toasted cashew pieces, basil and fresh cilantro.

Vegan Gumbo Recipe

Preparation time: 20 minutes

Cooking time: 8 hours

Servings: 4 to 6

Ingredients:

2 tbsp olive oil

1 yellow onion, finely chopped

1 green bell pepper, diced

2 stalks celery, diced

3 garlic cloves, minced

2 tbsp whole wheat flour

2 cups vegetable broth

14.5 oz. (1 can) diced tomatoes

15 oz. (1 can) kidney beans, rinsed and drained

8 oz. white mushrooms, quartered

1 small zucchini, cut into thick half moons

1 cup sliced okra, frozen

2 tbsp vegan Worcestershire sauce

1 tbsp Cajun seasoning

1 bay leaf

Pepper and salt to taste

For serving: Cooked Rice and hot sauce

Directions:

1. Pour 1 tbsp oil in a Dutch oven and heat over medium heat. Add the onion, celery, bell pepper, and garlic; cook for 8 to 10 minutes or until softened and about to turn brown.

2. Transfer cooked veggies to a 4 to 6 qt. slow cooker.

3. Place the Dutch oven to the stovetop; pour the remaining tbsp of oil into it. Add the flour while stirring it in. cook and stir often for 4 minutes or until it turns golden brown.

4. Pour the broth into the Dutch oven and bring to a boil; once the broth is boiling, pour it into the slow cooker. Add all of the remaining ingredients except cooked rice and hot sauce.

5. Cover and cook on low for 6 to 8 hours.

6. Remove the bay leaf once the gumbo is ready. Add pepper and salt to taste. Serve gumbo over rice with hot sauce.

Pumpkin Red Lentil Chili

This is the perfect chili for cold weather. It's hearty, thick and delicious.

Preparation time: 10 minutes

Cooking time: 8 hours

Servings: 6

Ingredients:

2 (15 oz) cans kidney beans, drained

2 cups vegetable broth

2 (15 oz.) cans fire-roasted diced tomatoes

1 cup dry red lentils

1 cup pumpkin puree

1 cup chopped yellow onion

1 medium jalapeno pepper, minced (remove seed before mincing to get a milder chili)

1 tbsp powdered cocoa

1 tbsp powdered chili

2 tsp cumin

½ tsp cinnamon

1/8 tsp cloves

1 tsp kosher salt

Optional toppings: Diced tomatoes, diced onions

Directions:

1. Pour all the ingredients into a 3 qt. or larger slow cooker, and then stir.

2. Cover and cook on low for 8 to 10 hours or on high for 4 to 5 hours or until lentils are soft and chili is hearty and thick.

3. Top with desired toppings. Serve.

Vegan White Bean Stew

This is a quick, easy and delicious vegan white bean stew, cooked in a slow cooker.

Preparation time: 20 minutes

Cooking time: 4 hours

Servings: 10 to 12

Ingredients:

2 lbs. white beans

2 large carrots, peeled and chopped

3 large celery stalks, diced

1 onion, diced

3 garlic cloves, minced

1 bay leaf

1 teaspoon dried rosemary

1 teaspoon thyme

1 teaspoon oregano

10 to 12 cups water

1 to 2 tablespoons salt (or more to taste)

Ground black pepper, to taste

28 oz. diced tomatoes

5 to 6 cups coarsely chopped spinach, kale, chard (or more)

For serving: Rice, bread or polenta

Directions:

1. Remove dirt and rinse beans in cool water several times. Pour rinsed beans into the slow cooker. Add the diced carrots, onions, celery, bay leaf, garlic, and dried herbs. Add the water (Use less for a thicker stew, more for more of a soup.)

2. Cover and cook on low for 8 to 10 hours or on high for 3-4 hours. Uncover the slow cooker; add pepper, diced tomatoes and salt.

3. Cook for 1 to 1½ hours, or until beans are very soft. (Add greens and tomatoes if beans are ready after the initial cooking time). Stir in the chopped beans and serve immediately.

3. Serve stew over steamy cooked rice, bread or polenta.

Cooking tips: Cooking time for beans depends on the freshness of beans. Great Northern Beans cook on high for 3 to 4 hours. Navy beans will take a little less time to cook while white kidney beans (Cannellini beans) will take even longer time to cook because they are larger.

Fire Roasted Chili

This spicy slow cooker chili combines a variety of beans, peppers and fire roasted tomatoes to produce a taste that is out of this world!

Preparation time: 20 minutes

Cooking time: 8 hours, 5 minutes

Servings: 6 to 8

Ingredients:

1 tbsp olive oil

1 large sweet yellow onion, finely chopped

½ red bell pepper, seeds removed and chopped

½ poblano pepper, seeded and chopped

2 garlic cloves, minced

3 tbsp tomato paste

1 tbsp powdered chili

28 oz. (1 can) crushed fire roasted tomatoes

15.5 oz. (1 can) Northern beans, rinsed and drained

15.5 oz. (1 can) pinto beans, rinsed and drained

15.5 oz. (1 can) kidney beans, rinsed and drained

1½ cups homemade vegetable broth

1 tsp salt

¼ tsp freshly ground black pepper

Directions:

1. Pour oil into shallow skillet and heat over medium heat. Pour in the onion, poblano pepper and red bell pepper. Cook until the onions become transparent and the peppers are slightly soft.

2. Add garlic and cook for 1 more minute. Add the tomato paste and powdered chili while stirring. Cook for 1 minute.

3. Remove the skillet from heat and transfer mixture to a 4 to 6 qt. slow cooker.

4. Pour in the fire roasted tomatoes, broth, beans, pepper and salt. Stir until properly mixed. Cover and cook on low for 7 - 8 hours.

Sweet "N" Spicy Veggie Curry

Preparation time: 30 minutes

Cooking time: 6 hour

Servings: 4 to 6

Ingredients:

2 tablespoons extra virgin olive oil

1 whole small onion

4 celery stalks, chopped

1/3 head cabbage, shredded

½ cup chopped baby carrots

1 whole sweet potato, diced

1 whole apple, chopped

½ can chick peas, rinsed and drained

2 ½ cups vegetable broth

½ can light coconut milk (to add later)

1 pinch pepper and salt (to add later)

Directions:

1. Pour all the ingredients into the slow cooker.

2. Cover and cook on low for 6 hours. Stir curry halfway through to make sure the veggies are evenly covered.

Coconut Butternut Squash & Chickpea Curry

Preparation time: 20 minutes

Cooking time: 6 hours, 30 minutes

Servings: 8

Ingredients:

2 ½ cups chopped butternut squash

1 ½ cups organic chick peas, dried

1 small onion, finely diced

2 garlic cloves, minced

13.5 oz. coconut milk, organic or light

1 bunch of fresh kale (or spinach), rinsed and roughly chopped

1 ½ cups shelled peas, fresh or frozen

1 to 2 large tomatoes, diced

3 cups water or vegetable broth

3 tbsp yellow powdered curry (or your own blend of spices)

1 tsp kosher salt

Handful of fresh cilantro, roughly chopped and divided

Directions:

1. Sort through the dry chickpeas and rinse. Cut off the squash skin, remove the seeds and cut into cubes about 1 inch square.

2. Pour all the ingredients except spinach and peas into the slow cooker. Cover and cook on high for 6 hours.

3. Add spinach and fresh peas when it's about 20 to 30 minutes before serving, and then stir.

4. If the soup is thin or too watery after cooking, do a quick mix of cornstarch and hot water. Pour 1 to 2 tbsp of the mixture into the slow cooker. Simmer for a bit longer to make soup thick.

5. Serve soup over brown jasmine or basmati rice. Top with basil, fresh cilantro, shredded coconut or mint.

Vegan Quinoa 'N' Black Bean Chili

Preparation time: 10 minutes

Cooking time: 3 hours

Servings: 4 to 5

Ingredients:

2 ¼ cups vegetable broth

½ cup quinoa, uncooked

15 oz. black beans

½ container of 28 oz. diced tomatoes

¼ cup chopped red bell pepper

¼ cup chopped green bell pepper

1 carrot, shredded

½ onion, chopped

2 garlic cloves

½ small sized chili pepper

2 tsp powdered chili

¼ tsp cayenne pepper

1 ½ tsp salt

1 tsp ground black pepper

1 tsp ground cumin

1 tsp oregano

½ cup corn kernels

For toppings: Avocado, chopped into chunks, shredded carrot and chopped green onions

Directions:

1. Pour broth, black beans, quinoa and tomatoes into the slow cooker. Stir to mix well.

2. Add the carrot, peppers, garlic, and onion. Stir and then add the remaining seasonings. Stir often to combine.

3. Cover and cook on low for 5 to 6 hours (monitor the last 30 minutes) or high for 2 ½ to 3 hours (monitor the last 30 minutes too).

4. Serve chili with preferred toppings.

Vegan Irish Stew

Preparation time: 10 minutes

Cooking time: 6 to 8 hours

Servings: 4

Ingredients:

1 tbsp olive oil

1 medium sweet yellow, white or red onion, diced

2 garlic cloves, minced

4 cups homemade vegetable broth at room temperature

1 tbsp nutritional yeast flakes

¾ cup apple juice or cider

¼ cup apple cider vinegar

3 large peeled potatoes, chopped into chunks

2 large peeled carrots, chopped into chunks

3 large ribs celery, diced into chunks

2 large peeled parsnips, chopped into chunks

3 tbsp pearl barley

½ tsp dried sage (or 3 fresh sage leaves finely chopped)

Pepper and salt to taste

1 bay leaf

½ cup thawed frozen peas

Optional toppings:

4 to 6 green onions, chopped

Fresh parsley, coarsely chopped

Directions:

1. Pour olive oil into a large sauté pan and heat over medium heat. Add garlic and onions, and then sauté for 5 minutes or until softened.

2. Transfer sautéed mixture into the slow cooker. Add broth and nutritional yeast; stir until nutritional yeast dissolves. Add the apple cider vinegar and apple.

3. Pour the remaining ingredients except green onions and peas into the slow cooker. Stir, cover and cook on low for 6 to 8 hours.

4. Add the peas during the last hour of cooking time.

5. Remove the bay leaf and spoon soup into serving bowls. Sprinkle chopped parsley and green onions generously over soup. Serve.

VEGETABLE MAIN DISHES

Vegan Fajitas

Preparation time: 20 minutes

Cooking time: 2 to 4 minutes

Servings: 8

Ingredients:

3 roma tomatoes, diced

4 oz. diced green chilies

1 large seeded green bell pepper, sliced

1 large seeded red bell pepper, sliced

1 medium onion, sliced thinly

1 ½ tbsp vegetable oil

2 tsp cumin

2 tsp powdered chili

½ tsp dried oregano

¼ tsp garlic salt

Directions:

1. Grease slow cooker with non-stick spray.

2. Pour all the ingredients into the slow cooker. Stir with a large spoon until the veggies are properly coated with spices and oil.

3. Cover and cook on low for 4 to 6 hours or on high for 2 hours.

4. Serve with warmed tortillas, avocado, black beans and vegan sour cream.

Greek Style Stuffed Peppers

This vegetarian stuffed pepper is easy to make. It comes out tender and delicious.

Preparation time: 15 minutes

Cooking time: 4 hours

Servings: 4

Ingredients:

4 large bell peppers

15 oz. (1 can) cannellini beans, rinsed and drained

4 oz. (1 cup) crumbled feta

½ cup couscous

4 scallions, thinly sliced, green and white parts set apart

1 garlic clove, minced

1 tsp dried oregano

Freshly ground pepper and coarse salt

For serving: Lemon wedges

Directions:

1. Slice a very thin layer from the base of each bell pepper so they sit flat. Slice off the tops of the bell pepper just below stem.

2. Discard stems; chop tops, and place in a medium-size bowl. Remove the seeds and ribs from peppers.

3. Pour beans, couscous, feta, oregano, scallion whites, and garlic into the bowl. Add pepper and salt. Toss to properly mix.

4. Stuff the peppers with the bean mixture. Place the stuffed peppers upright in the slow cooker. Cover and cook on high for 4 hours.

5. Sprinkle scallion greens over stuffed peppers. Serve with lemon wedges.

Quinoa-Lentil Taco Filling

Preparation time: 15 minutes

Cooking time: 8 hours

Servings: 6 tacos

Ingredients:

½ cup brown lentils

¼ cup quinoa, rinsed

2 cups water

2 garlic cloves, minced

½ tsp powdered chili

½ tsp smoked paprika

Pepper and salt to taste

6 gluten-free corn taco shells, soft or hard

Instructions:

1. Pour all the ingredients except pepper, taco shells and salt into a 1½ to 2 qt. slow cooker.

2. Cover and cook on low for 7 to 9 hours. Add pepper and salt to taste before serving.

3. Serve cooked mixture in taco shells topped with lettuce, salsa, tomatoes, or desired taco toppings.

Cooking tips: If cooking takes more 9 hours, add more liquid so it doesn't burn.

Sweet Potato Lentils

Preparation time: 20 minutes

Cooking time: 4 ½ hours

Servings: 6 to 8

Ingredients:

6 cups diced sweet potatoes (or 3 large sweet potatoes, diced)

3 cups vegetable broth

1 onion, chopped

4 garlic cloves, minced

2 tsp ground coriander

2 tsp garam masala

2 tsp powdered chili

½ tsp salt

1½ cups red lentils, uncooked

1 can coconut milk

1 cup water

Directions:

1. Pour sweet potatoes, onion, broth, garlic and spices into the slow cooker. Cover and cook on high for 3 hours or until veggies are tender.

2. Add lentils and stir once. Cover and cook on high for another 1½ hours.

3. Add the coconut milk while stirring. Add enough water to get desired consistency.

Vegan Chipotle Tacos

Preparation time: 20 minutes

Cooking time: 4 hours

Servings: 4

Ingredients:

2 (15 ounces) cans pinto beans, drained

1 cup corn kernels, fresh, frozen or canned

1 chipotle pepper in adobo sauce, chopped

6 oz. tomato paste

¾ cup chili sauce

1 tbsp powdered cocoa, unsweetened

1 tsp ground cumin

½ tsp ground cinnamon

½ tsp kosher salt

Directions:

1. Pour all the ingredients into the slow cooker.

2. Cover and cook on high for 1 ½ to 2 hours or on low for 3 to 4 hours.

3. Ladle cooked mixture on desired taco shells whether hard or soft.

4. Top with sliced romaine, lettuce, tomatoes, lime or avocado.

5. If desired, serve with beans and rice.

Cooking tips: Allow to cool to room temperature before storing in a rigid sided container before freezing. To reheat after freezing, place frozen meal in the refrigerator for 4 to 6 hours before serving. Then heat up the filling in a saucepan until properly heated. Serve.

Vegan Jambalaya

Preparation time: 30 minutes

Cooking time: 2 hours

Servings: 10

Ingredients:

6 oz. soy chorizo (opt.)

1 green bell pepper

1 cup okra

½ onion

3 celery ribs, diced (about 1½ cups)

2 garlic cloves

16 oz. diced tomatoes and green chilies

1½ cups vegetable broth

½ teaspoon paprika

¼ teaspoon salt

¼ teaspoon ground black pepper

¼ teaspoon cayenne pepper

3 cups cilantro rice, cooked

Directions:

1. Place the chorizo in a skillet and cook over medium-high heat. Allow until browned.

2. Transfer to a slow cooker.

3. Dice the bell pepper, onion, okra and celery; mince the garlic. Add diced and minced veggies in the slow cooker. Pour in the broth and diced tomatoes. Add the pepper and salt to taste. Stir until veggies are completely mixed.

4. Cover and cook on high for 2 hours or on low for 4 to 6 hours.

5. Add the cooked rice and mix.

Vegan Meat Loaf (Nut Loaf)

Preparation time: 20 minutes

Cooking time: 6 hours, 20 minutes

Servings: 4

Ingredients:

1 cup chopped pecans

1 cup chopped almonds

1 cup chopped cashews

1 medium onion, finely chopped

4 green onions, diced

4 large garlic cloves, chopped

1 medium peeled carrot, chopped

1 to 2 tablespoon of spice mix (equal mix of fennel, sage, rosemary, thyme, oregano)

2 teaspoons bay leaves or 2 bay leaves

1 teaspoon sea salt

½ teaspoon black pepper

¼ cup ground chia seeds

1 cup ground almonds

1 cup ground pecans

½ cup brown rice flour

¾ cup ground flax seeds

1/8 cup powdered arrowroot (or more flax seed)

2 cups vegetable broth

½ cup tomato paste

1 tablespoon balsamic vinegar

2 tablespoons molasses

Sea salt to taste

Directions:

1. Line the slow cooker with a foil or parchment paper. The loaf will be placed on it so it doesn't stick and easy to remove.

2. Pour chopped nuts into a large pan and toast on stove over medium-low heat for 8 to 10 minutes. Stir often, so it doesn't burn. The nuts are ready when they smell like cake.

3. Pour onions, green onions, garlic, carrots, celery, spices, flour, chia seeds, flax seeds, ground nuts and powdered arrow-root into a bowl, and then mix together.

4. Pour in the toasted nuts and mix completely. Add the broth and stir until the mixture slightly damp and evenly coated.

5. Transfer the mixture to the slow cooker, press the top down until it becomes smooth.

6. Cover the slow cooker and cook on low for 5 hours.

7. After the 5 hours cooking time, Place a pot on the stove and whisk in tomato paste, balsamic vinegar, molasses and sea salt, and then heat up over medium-high heat.

8. Spread mixture over the loaf and cook for another 1 hour.

9. Remove from the slow cooker and allow to cool for 10 minutes before slicing. Serve. Enjoy!

Cooking tips: For ground spices and seeds: pour them into a blender or coffee grinder and process.

Indian-Style Spiced Chickpeas 'N' Red Potatoes

Enjoy your dinner the Indian way. This recipe combines spices with chickpeas and potatoes to give a deliciously tasty weeknight dinner.

Preparation time: 20 minutes

Cooking time: 4 hours

Servings: 4 to 6

Ingredients:

2 tsp olive oil

2 cups diced yellow onion (or 1 medium yellow onion, diced)

2 tsp minced garlic cloves (or 2 medium cloves garlic, minced)

2 tsp ground coriander

2 tsp ground cumin

½ tsp garam masala

½ tsp ground ginger

¼ tsp turmeric

¼ tsp crushed red pepper flakes

1 tsp kosher salt

15 oz. diced tomatoes

2 tbsp tomato paste

1 cup vegetable broth

2 (15-oz.) cans chickpeas, drained and rinsed

1 lb. red potatoes, diced into about ½ -inch

1 lime

Small bunch fresh cilantro

Directions:

1. Sprinkle olive in a large sauté pan and heat up over medium heat. Add the onion and then cook while stirring often for 5 minutes or until it becomes soft and transparent.

2. Add the garlic, cumin, coriander, ground ginger, garam masala, red pepper flakes, turmeric and salt. Cook while stirring often for 1 minute.

3. Add the diced tomatoes, broth and tomato paste. Stir until properly mixed. Pour mixture into the slow cooker. Add the potatoes and chickpeas, and then stir.

4. Cover and cook on low for 8 to 10 hours or on high for 4 to 5 hours or until the potatoes soft or tender.

5. Scoop into serving bowls. Squeeze lime wedges on top and top with fresh cilantro. Serve.

Vegan Eggplant With Potatoes

Preparation time: 20 minutes

Cooking time: 2 hours, 30 minutes

Servings: 8

Ingredients:

10 to 12 cups diced eggplants (or 2 medium eggplants, trim off stem end and cut into ½ -inch)

1 large peeled Yukon Gold or Idaho potato, diced about ½ -inch

1 medium yellow or red onion, peeled and diced

1 teaspoon ginger paste (or fresh ginger root, grated)

6 peeled garlic cloves, roughly chopped

2 jalapeño chilies, seeded and minced

1 tablespoon ground cumin

1 tablespoon ground red chili pepper

1 tablespoon garam masala

1 teaspoon turmeric

¼ cup canola oil

1 tablespoon kosher salt, or to taste

1 to 2 tablespoon chopped fresh cilantro, to taste

Directions:

1. Pour eggplant, onion, potato, jalapeno peppers, ginger, cumin, garlic, ground chile pepper, turmeric, garam masala and oil into a 4 to 5 qt. slow cooker. Stir well until spices and oil is well distributed.

2. Cover and cook on high for 2 hours, stir after 1 hour.

3. After 2 hours of cooking, the eggplant should have collapsed and mixture should have reasonable amount of moisture.

4. Continue cooking on low for 30 minutes if there is still plenty of liquid in the slow cooker.

5. Add cilantro and salt to taste. (The salt added will bring out more moisture from the eggplant, so it's good to add salt at the very end.)

6. Allow to cool at room temperature and serve over rice. Topped with raita

Vegan 3-Bean Chili With Quinoa

Preparation time: 10 minutes

Cooking time: 5 hours

Servings: 8

Ingredients:

2 tablespoon powdered chili

1 tablespoon cumin

2 teaspoon paprika

½ teaspoon cayenne pepper

1 teaspoon salt (or more to taste)

14 oz. (1 can) black beans, drained and rinsed

14 oz. (1 can) pinto beans, drained and rinsed

14 oz. (1 can) red kidney beans, drained and rinsed

1 poblano pepper

1 red bell pepper

½ large white onion

1 cup frozen corn

1 large sweet potato

28 oz. (1 can) whole tomatoes

½ cup quinoa, raw

3.5 cups vegetable broth

Directions:

1. Combine all the spices in a bowl, mix and set aside.

2. Prepare the veggies: peel the potato and chop into small chunks; chop peppers into small pieces and dice the onion.

3. Pour beans, veggies, spices, quinoa, broth and tomatoes into the slow cooker.

4. Cover and cook on low for 4 to 6 hours.

5. Top with avocado, chopped fresh cilantro or green onions if desired. Serve.

Vegetable Succotash

This recipe combines your favorite summer vegetables of beans, peppers and eggplant. This can be served as a salad during summer.

Preparation time: 15 minutes

Cooking time: 4 hours

Servings: 4 to 6

Ingredients:

10 oz. (1 can) diced tomatoes in juice

½ cup vegetable broth

2 cups corn kernels

2 cups diced zucchini

1 cup sliced okra

1/3 cup diced white onion

3 garlic cloves, minced

½ tsp salt

¼ tsp ground black pepper

¼ tsp red pepper flakes

2 tbsp lemon juice

½ tsp hot sauce

½ tsp dried parsley (or 1 tbsp freshly chopped parsley)

Directions:

1. Set the slow cooker setting to low. Pour tomatoes and its juice, broth into the slow cooker.

2. Pour the corn, okra, zucchini, garlic and onion into the slow cooker. Sprinkle salt, red pepper flakes and black pepper over the mixture. Stir to mix well.

3. Cover and cook on low for 4 hours.

4. Before serving the succotash, whisk lemon juice and hot sauce together in a bowl. Add the parsley and stir properly.

5. When the succotash his ready, sprinkle the lemon juice mixture over the succotash and stir. Spoon into individual bowls and serve.

PASTA, RISOTTO AND GRAINS

Spanish Vegan Rice

Preparation time: 5 minutes

Cooking time: 3 hours

Servings: 10

Ingredients:

1 cup uncooked long grain rice

1 cup water

½ cup diced onion

½ cup finely chopped green bell pepper

2 garlic cloves, minced

1 tsp powdered chili

1 tsp ground cumin

½ tsp salt

14.5 oz. (1 can) diced tomatoes, undrained

Directions:

1. Grease a 4 qt. slow cooker with cooking spray. Pour all the ingredients into the slow cooker and mix.

2. Cover and cook on low for 2 to 3 hours, or until the rice is soft and the liquid absorbed.

Mexican-Style Rice 'N' Beans

Preparation time: 20 minutes

Cooking time: 3 hours

Servings: 4

Ingredients:

1 cup uncooked brown long rice

1 jar salsa

15 oz. (1 can) black beans

1 packet taco seasoning

1 cup vegetable broth

2 garlic cloves, minced

1 jalapeno, seeded and minced (opt.)

Directions:

1. Rinse the beans and rice.

2. Pour all the ingredients into the slow cooker. Stir, cover and cook on high for 3 hours.

Cooking tips: To be creative, you may add butternut squash or corn, sprinkle vegan cheese over rice and beans in the slow cooker about 10 minutes before the cooking time finishes. Serve meal as a dip with chips. Enjoy!

Southern Spiced Chickpeas And Grits

Preparation time: 15 minutes

Cooking time: 16 hours

Servings: 4½ cups

Ingredients:

1 ½ cups (16 oz.) cooked chickpeas

1 cup chopped bell pepper

1 ½ (14.5 oz.) cups diced tomatoes

½ cup water

2 tsp Cajun spice blend

¼ to ½ tsp powdered chipotle

2 garlic cloves, minced

Few dashes smoked salt or liquid smoke

Tabasco or other hot sauce, (opt.)

Pepper and salt to taste

For the Grits:

½ cup white or yellow grits

1 cup almond milk, unsweetened (or any non-diary milk)

1 cup water

1 vegetable bouillon cube

Pepper and salt to taste

Directions:

1. Pour all the ingredients except pepper and salt into the slow cooker. Cover and cook on low for 7 to 9 hours.

2. Add pepper and salt to taste before serving. If desired, add more Cajun seasoning, liquid smoke or chipotle. Adjust pepper and salt to taste.

3. To prepare grit: Pour all the ingredients for grit into a slow cooker. Cover and cook on low for 7 to 9 hours.

4. Serve spiced chickpeas over grits

Note: recipe for grits makes 2 cup.

Vegan Artichoke Pasta

Preparation time: 15 minutes

Cooking time: Low: 6 to 8 hrs; High: 3-4 hours

Servings: 6

Ingredients:

Cooking spray, nonstick

3 (14 ½ oz.) cans diced tomatoes with garlic, oregano and basil

28 oz. (2 cans) artichoke hearts, drained and quartered

6 garlic cloves, minced

½ cup coconut milk or soy cream

12 oz. dried fettucine, linguine, or desired pasta

Ripe olives, pitted and sliced (or sliced pimiento-stuffed green olives) (opt.)

Crumbled Vegan tofu feta cheese (opt.)

Directions:

1. Grease the inside of a 3 ½ to 4-qt. slow cooker with cooking spray. Drain 2 cans of diced tomatoes (leave the 3rd can for later use).

2. Pour the drained and undrained tomatoes, garlic and artichoke into the greased slow cooker. Stir.

3. Cover the slow cooker and cook on high for 3 to 4 hours or on low for 6 to 8 hours. Add the coconut milk or soy cream, stir and then allow to heat through for 5 minutes.

4. While the sauce is cooking, cook the pasta according to package instructions and drain.

5. Serve the sauce over steamy cooked pasta. Top with vegan cheese or olives if desired.

Veggie Ziti

Preparation time: 10 minutes

Cooking time: 3 hours

Servings: 6 to 8

Ingredients:

1 lb. uncooked ziti pasta

2 cups grated zucchini (or 1 large zucchini, grated)

1 cup grated carrot (or 1 large carrot, grated)

1 cup diced red bell pepper (or 1 red bell pepper, diced)

1 cup diced onion (or 1 small onion, finely diced)

1 garlic clove, minced

28 oz. (1 can) diced tomatoes

15 oz. (1 can) tomato puree (or sauce without seasonings)

1 tsp salt

½ cup grated vegan parmesan cheese

3 cups grated vegan mozzarella cheese, divided

Directions:

1. Pour all the ingredients except 1 cup of vegan mozzarella cheese into a slow cooker. Stir until properly mixed.

2. Sprinkle the remaining 1 cup vegan mozzarella cheese evenly on top of the pasta mixture.

3. Cover the slow cooker and cook on low for 6 hours or on high for 3 hours.

Veggies 'N' Spaghetti

This is an easy slow cooker spaghetti meal.

Preparation time: 10 minutes

Cooking time: 2 hours

Servings: 5

Ingredients:

½ package brown rice spaghetti (or desired pasta)

2 cups water

1 green pepper chopped

½ onion, diced

2 garlic cloves, minced

1 red pepper chopped

5 to 7 mushrooms, sliced

3 cups diced tomatoes (or 28 oz. of diced tomatoes)

2 tablespoons chopped fresh basil

2 tablespoons chopped fresh parsley

Sea salt to taste

Directions:

1. Pour all the ingredients except parsley, basil and pasta into the slow cooker. Cover and cook on low for about 30 minutes.

2. Increase slow cooker setting to high and cook for another 1 ½ hours or until the onions becomes tender.

3. Pour in the pasta when it's about 20 minutes before cooking time elapse.

4. Add the parsley and basil when it's about 5 minutes before spaghetti is ready.

Cooking tips: Add arrowroot or gluten free cornstarch to thicken sauce if it's watery or thin. Store meal in a refrigerator for up to a week.

Chickpea 'N' Barley Risotto

Preparation time: 10 minutes

Cooking time: 2 hours, 40 minutes

Servings: 4

Ingredients:

1 ½ tbsp extra virgin olive oil

3 peeled carrots, chopped

3 garlic cloves, minced

½ head cauliflower, cut into small florets

½ small yellow onion, minced

4 sprigs fresh thyme

1 ¼ cups pearl barley, rinsed

15.5 oz. (1 can) garbanzo beans, rinsed and drained

2 ½ cups vegetable broth

1¼ cups water

½ tsp kosher salt

¼ tsp ground black pepper

1 ½ tbsp fresh lemon juice

1/3 cup grated vegan parmesan cheese

3 tbsp chopped fresh parsley

Directions:

1. Pour oil into a large saucepan and heat over medium-high heat. Pour in the carrots, cauliflower, garlic and onion. Cook for 5 minutes or until veggies begin to soften, stirring often.

2. Add barley and thyme while stirring it in. Cook for 2 minutes, stirring consistently.

3. Transfer the mixture to the slow-cooker. Add the garbanzo beans, water, broth, pepper and salt, and then stir.

4. Cover and cook on high 2 to 2 ½ hours or until the barley is soft and enough liquid is absorbed.

5. Remove the thyme sprigs from the slow cooker and discard. Stir in the lemon juice. Serve meal in warm bowls topped with parsley and vegan cheese.

Fennel With Barley Risotto

This healthy slow cooked fennel with barley risotto is an excellent choice for a fiber rich meal. This is an alternative to the stovetop risotto and it doesn't require much stirring.

Preparation time: 30 minutes

Cooking time: 3 hours

Servings: 5

Ingredients:

2 tsp fennel seeds

1 large fennel bulb, cored and diced (or 2 small fennel bulbs)

2 tbsp chopped fronds

1 cup pearl barley (or short-grain brown rice)

1 small carrot, diced

1 large shallot, chopped

2 garlic cloves, minced

4 cups vegetable broth

1 to 1 ½ cups water, divided

1/3 cup dry white wine

2 cups French-cut green beans, frozen

½ cup grated vegan parmesan cheese

1/3 cup black olives, pitted, oil-cured and roughly chopped

1 tbsp freshly grated lemon zest

Freshly ground pepper, to taste

Directions:

1. Grease a 4-qt. or larger slow cooker with cooking spray.

2. Use the bottom of a saucepan to crush fennel seeds. Pour the fennel seeds, rice or barley, diced fennel, carrot, garlic and shallot into the slow cooker. Pour in the broth, wine and 1 cup water. Stir until well combined.

3. Cover the slow cooker and cook on high for 2 ½ hours or on low for 3 ½ hours, or until the barley (or rice) is soft and chewy, and the risotto is creamy and thick.

4. Before serving, cook the green beans according to package directions, and then drain.

5. Turn off the slow cooker. Pour the cooked green beans, olives, vegan parmesan, pepper and lemon zest into the risotto. Stir.

6. Add ½ cup of water to the risotto if it looks dry, and then stir. Sprinkle chopped fennel fronds on top. Serve.

Preparation tips: Prepare the fennel, shallot, carrot and garlic in separate containers and store in a fridge. Mix broth, wine and 1 cup water in a container and refrigerate for 1 day.

Cleaning tips: Use a slow cooker liner or a parchment pepper to ease cleanup. These liners are disposable, heat-resistant and fit neatly inside the slow cooker. It helps prevent food from sticking to the sides and bottom of your slow cooker.

Vegan Corn Risotto

Preparation time: 10 minutes

Cooking time: 2 hours, 50 minutes

Servings: 5

Ingredients:

1¼ cup Arborio rice

1 tablespoon olive oil

1 tablespoon coconut oil

1 teaspoon onion flakes

4 garlic cloves, chopped

4 cups vegetable broth

16 oz. frozen corn

1 teaspoon salt

¼ to ½ teaspoon cayenne pepper, (or more to taste)

¼ cup soy cream or coconut milk

½ cup shredded vegan parmesan cheese

Directions:

1. Pour olive oil into a 4 qt. slow cooker. Add the rice and onion flakes, and then swirl.

2. Add the chopped garlic, cayenne pepper and salt. Add the broth and frozen corn. Stir until properly mixed. Add a few drops of coconut oil.

3. Cover the slow cooker and cook on high for 2 hours. Check meal every 45 minutes. When done, rice should be tender and the liquid absorbed.

4. Turn off the slow cooker. Add soy cream or coconut milk, vegan cheese. Cover the slow cooker for 5 minutes, or until cheese completely melts. Serve.

Vegan Brown Rice 'N' Lentil Tacos

Preparation time: 10 minutes

Cooking time: 4 hours

Servings: 4

Ingredients:

1 cup lentils

½ cup brown rice

1 onion, diced

6 garlic cloves, minced

4 ½ cups water

2 tbsp powdered chili

½ tsp powdered onion

¼ tsp red pepper flakes

½ tsp paprika

2 tsp cumin

1½ teaspoons salt

½ teaspoon black pepper

Directions:

1. Pour all the ingredients into the slow cooker. Stir to mix well.

2. Cover the slow cooker and cook on high for 4 hours. Stir once during the last hour of the cooking time. Serve.

ONE POT MEALS AND CASSEROLES

Vegetable Casserole

Preparation time: 20 minutes

Cooking time: 2 to 6 hours, depending on heat

Servings: 8

Ingredients:

2 (19 oz.) can cannellini beans

19 oz. (1 can) fava or garbanzo beans

¼ cup basil pesto

1 medium onion, chopped

4 garlic cloves, minced

1 ½ tsp dried Italian seasoning

16 oz. (1 pkg.) cooked plain polenta, cut in ½ inch-thick slices and refrigerated

1 large tomato, thinly sliced

8 oz. (2 cups) shredded Italian cheese blend

2 cups fresh spinach

1 cup torn radicchio

Directions:

1. Rinse the beans and drain. Pour the beans, onion, 2 tbsp of pesto, Italian seasoning and garlic into a large bowl. Stir until completely mixed.

2. Layer ½ of the bean mixture, ½ of the polenta and ½ of the cheese blend in a 4 to 5 qt. slow cooker. Pour in the remaining beans and polenta.

3. Cover the slow cooker and cook on high for 2 to 2 ½ hours or on low for 4 to 6 hours. Pour in the tomato, spinach, remaining cheese blend and radicchio.

4. Mix the remaining pesto and 1 tbsp water together.

4. Sprinkle pesto mixture over casserole. Uncover and allow to stand for 5 minutes.

Vegan Cheesy Enchilada

This is a cheesy and protein filled slow cooker meal. It's easy to make; just throw in the ingredients, set it and forget it.

Preparation time: 5 minutes

Cooking time: 4 hours

Servings: 4 to 6

Ingredients:

15 oz. (1 can) black beans, drained and rinsed

15 oz. (1 can) yellow corn, drained and rinsed

2 (15 oz.) cans of mild or medium red enchilada sauce, divided

15 oz. (1 can) of diced fire roasted tomatoes and green chilies

1 cup quinoa, uncooked

½ cup water

4 oz. vegan sour cream

¼ tsp black pepper

1 tsp salt

1 cup grated vegan Mexican cheese

119

Optional toppings: diced tomatoes, chopped cilantro, vegan sour cream, diced avocado

Directions:

1. Pour beans, corn, tomatoes and chilies, 1 can of enchilada sauce, quinoa, vegan sour cream, water, pepper and salt into the slow cooker. Stir until properly mixed.

2. Pour in the remaining can of enchilada sauce; sprinkle vegan cheese on top. Cover the slow cooker and cook on high for 4-5 hours or on low for 5-7 hours.

3. Remove the slow cooker lid, place tomatoes, vegan sour cream, cilantro, avocados on top. Serve.

Cooking tips: For more flavors, add 1 tsp each of powdered garlic and cumin.

One Pot Mexican-Style Brown Rice 'N' Beans With Avocados

This meal is full of spices and jalapeno and salsa flavors. Garnish casserole with vegan cheese and avocado for a hearty meal.

Preparation time: 20 minutes

Cooking time: 3 hours

Servings: 6

Ingredients:

2 garlic cloves, minced

½ jalapeno, minced

1 ¼ cup brown rice

2 cups vegetable broth

4 oz. (1 can) green chilies

14.5 oz. (1 can) black beans, rinsed and drained

1 ½ cups salsa or picante sauce

1 cup corn, frozen

1 teaspoon powdered chili

1 teaspoon cumin

½ teaspoon black pepper

½ teaspoon salt

1 bay leaf

1 ½ cups grated vegan cheddar cheese

1/3 cup chopped cilantro leaves

½ cup vegan sour cream

1 avocado, diced

Directions:

1. Pour garlic, rice, jalapeno, chilies, broth, beans, corn, salsa, powdered chili, cumin, salt, pepper and bay leaf into the slow cooker. Stir until well combined.

2. Cover the slow cooker and cook on high for 3 hours, or until the rice is soft.

3. Remove bay leaf from the slow cooker and discard. Sprinkle vegan cheese on top and let it melt for some minutes.

4. Top each serving with cilantro, vegan sour cream and avocados.

One Pot Vegetable Casserole

Preparation time: 30 minutes

Cooking time: 4 hours

Servings: 4 to 6

Ingredients:

14.5 oz. (1 can) unsalted tomato sauce

1 tbsp Italian herb blend

1 tsp salt

¼ tsp black pepper

1 large carrot, sliced

½ cup corn, frozen

½ cup peas, frozen

4 russet potatoes, sliced

2 large zucchini, sliced

1 ½ cups shredded vegan cheese

Directions:

1. Combine tomato sauce, pepper, carrots, herb blend, corn, peas and salt in a medium bowl.

2. Grease the inside of the slow cooker with a non-stick cooking spray. Spread potatoes on a single layer, overlapping it a little on the bottom of the slow cooker. Sprinkle pepper and salt on top.

3. In the same way, spread the zucchini on a single lager over the potatoes. Sprinkle pepper and salt on top.

4. Pour the 1/3 of the tomato sauce mixture on top, and then sprinkle ½ cup of vegan cheese on top.

5. Repeat the process two more times to get a total of three layers.

6. Cover the slow cooker and cook on high 3 ½ to 4 hours.

Hash Brown Casserole

Preparation time: 10 minutes

Cooking time: 4 hours

Servings: 10-12

Ingredients:

2 cups vegan sour cream

10.75 oz condensed cream of mushroom soup

½ cup of chopped onions

32 oz frozen hash brown potatoes, thawed

2 cups vegan cheese, shredded

¼ tsp salt

½ tsp black pepper

Directions:

1. Mix the cream of mushroom, onions, vegan cheese, salt, vegan sour cream and pepper in a bowl. Slowly stir in the hash brown potatoes until properly coated.

2. Grease the slow cooker with cooking spray. Using a spoon, scoop the potato mixture into the slow cooker and cover. Cook on high for 1½ hours and then on low for another 2½ hours.

Vegan Broccoli Casserole

Preparation time: 20 minutes

Cooking time: 4 hours

Servings: 5

Ingredients:

2 lbs. fresh broccoli, washed and trimmed

1/3 cup wheat flour

¼ teaspoon kosher salt

¼ teaspoon black pepper

½ teaspoon ground mustard

1 cup almond milk (or any non-diary milk)

1 cup vegetable broth

1 cup shredded vegan white cheese

¼ vegan parmesan cheese (or more)

Directions:

1. Wash and trim the broccoli.

2. Combine wheat flour, pepper, dried mustard and salt in a large mixing bowl. Add the broccoli to the mixture and toss. Pour broccoli mixture into a 4 qt. slow cooker.

3. Pour in 1 cup of the vegan cheese, veggie broth and almond milk.

4. Cover and cook on high for 3 to 4hours or on low for 6 hours or until the broccoli is tender and its edges begin to turn brown.

5. Top casserole with vegan parmesan cheese.

Slow Cooked Eggplants

This is an ideal meal for night time. It's packed with summer flavors and easy to prepare.

Preparation time: 15 minutes

Cooking time: 8 hours

Servings: 6

Ingredients:

4 tablespoons olive oil

1 red onion, sliced

2 garlic cloves, crushed

1.1 lb. eggplants, sliced into 1 1/2 inch lengthways thick slices

2 to 3 medium size tomatoes, quartered

1 small fennel bulb, sliced

1.8 oz. sundried tomatoes

1 teaspoon coriander seeds

For dressing:

Small bunch flat leaf parsley, coarsely chopped

Small bunch basil, coarsely chopped

Small bunch chives, roughly chopped

2 tablespoons olive oil

1 lemon, juiced

2 teaspoons capers

For topping:

2/3 cup vegan feta cheese

1/3 cup toasted flaked almonds

To serve: Crusty bread

Directions:

1. Pour ½ of the olive oil into the slow cooker, add the onions and garlic.

2. Brush the remaining olive oil on the sliced eggplants.

3. Place the eggplants on top of the onions in the slow cooker. Place the tomatoes, sundried tomatoes and fennel slices around the eggplants. Sprinkle coriander seeds on top, and then season with pepper and salt to taste.

4. Cover and cook on low for 6 to 8 hours or until the eggplants are tender.

5. Once they are ready, pour all the dressing ingredients into a blender or food processor; blend until smooth.

6. Spoon cooked vegetables into a serving dish. Sprinkle dressing mixture on top.

7. Top with crumbled vegan feta cheese and flaked almonds. Serve with crusty bread on the side.

Mexican Enchilada Casserole

Prepare a delicious enchilada casserole the Mexican style. Allow your slow cooker do all the work.

Preparation time: 10 minutes

Cooking time: 5 hours

Servings: 5

Ingredients:

4 cups chopped veggies (any veggies of your choice)

8 corn tortillas

3 cups black beans

1.5 teaspoons cumin

1 teaspoon paprika

1 teaspoon cayenne pepper

1 cup shredded vegan Mexican cheese

1 can enchilada sauce

Directions:

1. Chop the veggies into pieces of same size

2. Grease the slow cooker with a cooking spray or line with a slow cooker liner.

3. Cut corn tortillas into strips and spread 1/3 of the strips on the bottom of the slow cooker. Top corn strips with 1/3 of the vegetables. Pour 1 cup of black beans on top followed by 1/3 can of enchilada sauce and then 1/3 cup of the vegan cheese.

4. Repeat the process two more times but don't add cheese on the very top layer.

5. Cover and cook on low for 4 hours.

6. Add the remaining vegan cheese and top with salsa and avocado. Serve warm.

Cooking tips: For the veggies: you can use sweet potato, mushrooms, red peppers and corn or any desired veggies.

Vegan Chinese Hot Pot

Preparation time: 20 minutes

Cooking time: 8 hours

Servings: 4

Ingredients:

1 small yellow onion, chopped

1 large carrot, cut in half lengthwise and sliced thinly on a diagonal

1 celery stalk, sliced thinly on a diagonal

6 oz. (1 can) sliced water chestnuts, drained

2 garlic cloves, finely minced

1 teaspoon peeled and grated fresh ginger

¼ teaspoon red pepper flakes

5 ½ cups vegetable stock

1 tablespoon tamari

8 oz. of extra-firm tofu, drained and diced

1 oz. snow peas, strings trimmed and cut into 1-inch pieces

4 oz. of fresh shiitake mushrooms, stemmed and caps sliced thinly

3 scallions, chopped

½ teaspoon toasted sesame oil or Chinese hot oil

Directions:

1. Combine onion, celery, carrot, garlic, water chestnuts, ginger and red pepper flakes in a 4 qt. slow cooker. Pour in tamari and vegetable stock.

2. Cover the slow cooker and cook on low for 8 hours.

3. When its 20 minutes before cooking time elapse, add the mushrooms, tofu, scallions and snow peas. Sprinkle sesame oil or Chinese hot oil on top.

4. Cover the slow cooker and cook until the snow peas and mushrooms are soft. Serve immediately.

Vegan One Pot Enchilada Pasta

Prepare simple and creamy enchilada pasta in your slow cooker. Hmmm yummy!

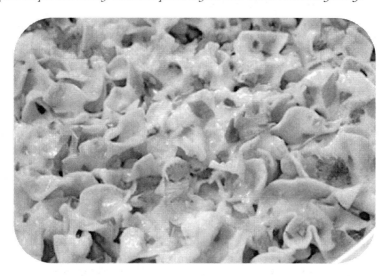

Preparation time: 10 minutes

Cooking time: 8 hours

Servings: 6

Ingredients:

14.5 oz. (1 can) fire roasted diced tomatoes

10 oz. (1 can) mild enchilada sauce

4.5 oz. (1 can) chopped green chilies, drained

½ cup vegetable broth (or more as needed)

1 cup corn kernels, frozen roasted or canned

1 cup canned black beans, drained and rinsed

Kosher salt to taste

Freshly ground black pepper to taste

4 oz. Vegan cream cheese, cubed

2 cups orzo pasta, uncooked

2 tbsp chopped fresh cilantro leaves

Directions:

1. Pour diced tomatoes, chilies, broth, enchilada sauce, corn and black beans into a slow cooker. Add pepper and salt to taste. Stir until properly mixed. Top with vegan cream cheese.

2. Cover the slow cooker and cook on high for 3 to 4 hours or on low for 7 to 8 hours. Remove the lid and stir until the vegan cream cheese is well mixed. Add the pasta.

3. Cover and cook on high for another 15 to 30 minutes. Pour in more veggie broth until the desired consistency is achieved.

4. If desired, garnish with cilantro. Serve immediately.

SIDE DISHES

Vegan Madras Lentils

Preparation time: 10 minutes

Cooking time: 4 hours

Servings: 4

Ingredients:

2 cups of cooked lentils

2 cups of canned tomato sauce

½ of a large onion, finely chopped

1 large Yukon Gold or Russet potato, peeled and cubed

½ cup of coconut milk, unsweetened

3 tablespoons coconut oil

3 garlic cloves, minced

½ teaspoon kosher salt

½ teaspoon dried oregano

½ teaspoon cumin

Red pepper flakes + freshly ground black pepper to taste

Directions:

1. Pour all the ingredients into the slow cooker.

2. Cover and cook on high for 3 ½ to 4 hours. Once done, taste and adjust salt and pepper to taste.

3. Sprinkle parsley on top. Serve over quinoa, rice or with green salad.

Spiced Pear Applesauce

Preparation time: 20 minutes

Cooking time: 6 hours

Servings: 6

Ingredients:

4 medium-size apples, peeled, cored, and chopped into large chunks

4 medium-size pears, peeled, cored, and chopped into large chunks

1 teaspoon lemon juice

5 teaspoons brown sugar

1 cinnamon stick

1 teaspoon vanilla extract

½ teaspoon ground ginger

½ teaspoon ground cardamom

½ teaspoon ground cloves

Directions:

1. Pour all the ingredients into the slow cooker. Cover and cook on low for 6 hours.

2. Remove the cinnamon stick from the slow cooker. To get a chunkier sauce, remove half of the apple and pear chunks with a slotted spoon. To get a thinner sauce, do not remove any fruit.

3. For chunkier sauce: Puree the fruit in the slow cooker with an immersion blender until smooth. Pour in the removed fruits and stir. For thin sauce: Allow the fruit to cool then blend until smooth.

Vegan Wild Rice Medley

Preparation time: 10 minutes

Cooking time: 4 hours

Servings: 6 to 8

Ingredients:

2 ½ cups vegetable broth

1 cup wild rice

2 garlic cloves, minced

1 medium onion, finely chopped

1 large carrot, diced

1 stalk celery, finely diced

2 tbsp dried porcini

½ tsp dried chervil

Black pepper

Directions:

1. Pour all the ingredients into the slow cooker, and then stir.

2. Cover and cook on low for 4 hours. Check to see, if the kernels are open and soft. If they are not, cover the slow cooker and continue cooking until they are open and tender. Check every 15 minutes, so they don't overcook. Stir together and serve hot.

Cooking tips: You can substitute the dried chervil for parsley. The rice cooking time depends on the slow cooker.

Vegan Refried Beans

This recipe tastes way better than the canned version. Enjoy your refried beans prepared in your slow cooker. Delicious!

Preparation time: 5 minutes

Cooking time: 8 hours

Servings: 4

Ingredients:

2 lbs. (5 cups) dried pinto beans, sorted and rinsed

1 medium to large yellow onion, diced

3 garlic cloves, minced

2 tsp of salt (or more to taste)

2 tsp ground black pepper

1 tsp ground powdered cumin

½ tsp crushed red pepper flakes (more or less to taste)

¼ tsp smoked paprika

9 cups of water (or more)

Directions:

1. Pour all the ingredients into the slow cooker and then stir to properly mix.

2. Cover and cook on high for 6 to 8 hours or until the beans are soft and can be mashed easily. Add more water if required during cooking.

3. Strain the beans in a large bowl and reserve the liquid. Mash the beans with a potato masher. Pour in the reserved liquid and stir until the desired consistency is achieved. Serve.

4. Cool and store in a refrigerator in portions.

Garlicky Mashed Cauliflower

Preparation time: 10 minutes

Cooking time: High: 2 to 3 hours; Low: 4 to 6 hours

Servings: 4 to 6

Ingredients:

1 head of cauliflower

3 cups water

4 large peeled garlic cloves

1 teaspoon salt

1 bay leaf

1 tablespoon applesauce

Almond milk or coconut milk

Pepper and Salt

Directions:

1. Trim the cauliflower into florets and then pour into the slow cooker. Add in water, garlic, salt and bay leaf.

2. Cover and cook on low for 4 to 6 hours or on high for 2 to 3 hours.

3. Remove the bay leaf and garlic cloves. Drain the water. Add in the applesauce.

4. Mash the cauliflower with a potato masher or use an immersion blender to make it creamy. Add a tbsp of coconut or almond milk at a time if required.

5. Add pepper and salt to taste. Serve with green onions and chives.

Vegan Saag Aloo

Preparation time: 5 minutes

Cooking time: 3 hours

Servings: 3 to 4

Ingredients:

22.9 oz. potatoes, peeled and cut into 1 inch chunks

½ onion, thinly sliced

¼ cup water

½ vegetable stock cube, crumbled

1 tablespoon oil

½ teaspoon cumin

½ teaspoon ground coriander

½ teaspoon garam masala

½ teaspoon powdered hot chili

Black pepper

16 oz. fresh spinach, coarsely chopped

Directions:

1. Pour potato chunks into the slow cooker. Add the sliced onion, crumbled stock cube, water, spices, oil and enough black pepper.

2. Top with big handfuls of fresh spinach. If it doesn't fit, add few and the rest later when it has wilted.

3. Cover and cook on medium or high for 3 hours, or until the potato is tender. Stir every 1 hour. The cooking time depends on how big your potato chunks are.

Vegan Mashed Potatoes

Preparation time: 10 minutes

Cooking time: 4 to 8 hours

Servings: 1

Ingredients:

1 russet potato, cubed

Water

2 tablespoons olive oil (or more)

½ teaspoon minced garlic (opt.)

¼ teaspoon thyme

Almond or coconut milk, unsweetened

Directions:

1. Pour the cubed potatoes into the slow cooker. Add enough water to barely cover the bottom of the slow cooker.

2. Cover and cook on high for 4 to 5 hours or on low for 6 to 8 hours.

3. Add the almond milk, garlic, olive oil and thyme.

4. Mix together with a hand mixer until desired consistency is achieved. Add more olive oil and milk to get creamier mashed potatoes.

Cooking tips: Start with 2 tablespoons of milk, then add more to get a creamier consistency.

Vegan Caramelized Onions

Preparation time: 10 minutes

Cooking time: 2 to 6 hours

Servings: 2

Ingredients:

2 onions or more

Olive oil

Directions:

1. Cut the onions and pour into a slow cooker.

2. Sprinkle olive oil on top.

3. Cover and cook on high for 2 to 3 hours or on low for 5 to 6 hours. Stir every 1 hour.

4. Serve on favorite dish. Enjoy!

5. Refrigerate leftovers.

Vegan Corn Cob

Preparation time: 10 minutes

Cook Time: 2 to 4 hours

Servings: 4

Ingredients:

6 corn on the cob (more or less)

4 tablespoon olive oil or coconut oil (or more if required)

1 tablespoon minced garlic

1 teaspoon Italian seasonings

Foil (opt.)

Directions:

1. Shuck and rinse the corn and remove the silk strands.

2. Combine olive oil, garlic and Italian seasoning in a small bowl.

3. Place the corn cob on the foil, if you are using a foil.

4. Sprinkle spoonful of olive oil mixture on each cob.

5. Wrap the corn in foil and place in the slow cooker.

6. Cover and cook on high for 2 hours or on low for 4 hours.

Cooking tips: If you want to keep the corn in the slow cooker on warm; make sure to rotate the corn often to avoid burning.

Vegan Potato French Fries

Preparation time: 10 minutes

Cooking time: 3 to 5 hours

Servings: 4

Ingredients:

7 cups scrubbed and sliced in wedges potatoes, leave the skin on

1/3 cup olive oil

2 tablespoons powdered garlic

2 tablespoons Italian seasoning

1 tablespoon paprika

1 teaspoon pepper

Salt to taste

Directions:

1. Pour the scrubbed and sliced potatoes into the slow cooker.

2. Add the olive oil, and then stir. Sprinkle seasoning on top.

3. Cover and cook on high for 3 hours or on low for 5 hours, or until potatoes are soft in the middle of the fry. Stir every 1 hour or ½ an hour.

Dairy-Free Slow Cooker Dressing Or Stuffing

Preparation time: 20 minutes

Cooking time: 3 hours

Servings: 4

Ingredients:

12 cups gluten-free bread, cubed

2 cups homemade vegetable broth (or more)

2 tablespoons olive oil or grape seed (opt.)

2 celery stalks, finely chopped

2 carrots, diced

1 medium onion, diced

1 apple, diced with skins

2 tbsp sage

1 tbsp thyme

1 tsp salt, or to taste

Directions:

1. If preferred, toast the cubed bread lightly on a baking sheet for 5 to 10 minutes at 200°F in the oven. (This is optional)

2. If preferred, for more flavor; pour 2 tbsp of olive oil in a saucepan, and then sauté celery, onion and carrots until the onions are transparent. (This is optional)

3. Pour all the ingredients into a big mixing bowl. Grease the slow cooker.

4. Pour mixture into the slow cooker.

5. Cover and cook on high for 1 hour, and then stir together. For more moist, add ½ cup broth to the slow cooker. Note that, the slow cooker retains moist when it's covered, so do not add too much broth.

6. Reduce slow cooker heat to low and cook for another 2 hours. Stir every 1 hour. Serve and enjoy!

DESSERTS AND DRINKS

Coconut - Almond Rice Pudding

Preparation time: 10 minutes

Cooking time: 2 to 4 hours

Servings: 4 to 5

Ingredients:

½ cup basmati rice, (white or brown)

1 can light coconut milk

1 cup vanilla almond milk, unsweetened

¼ – ½ cup water (more or less)

½ tsp vanilla extract

¼ tsp almond extract

½ tsp ground cinnamon

¼ tsp ground nutmeg

½ cup raisins

¼ cup chopped almonds, toasted

¼ cup shredded coconut

¼ cup maple syrup, divided

Directions:

1. Turn on the slow cooker.

2. Pour rice, almond milk, coconut milk, almond extract, vanilla extract, nutmeg and cinnamon into the slow cooker. Add little water if needed.

3. Cover and cook on low for 4 hours or on high for 2 to 2 ½ hours.

4. Once done, add the raisons, coconut and almonds, and then mix. Spoon rice pudding into four serving bowls. Sprinkle ½ to 1 tbsp of maple syrup on top followed by little coconut flakes.

5. Serve and enjoy!

Vegan Scalloped Peaches

Preparation time: 10 minutes

Cooking time: 2 hours

Servings: 8

Ingredients:

8 peaches, sliced

1 cup sugar

½ tsp ground cinnamon

½ tsp ground cloves

¼ cup olive oil or coconut oil

For serving: Vegan vanilla ice cream

Directions:

1. Pour peaches, cinnamon, sugar, cloves and olive oil into the bowl of a 4 qt. slow cooker. Toss lightly to mix well.

2. Cover and cook on low for 1 ½ to 2 hours. Serve hot with a scoop of the vegan ice cream.

Creamy Vegan Hot Chocolate

Preparation time: 5 minutes

Cooking time: 1 hour, 30 minutes

Servings: 4 cups

Ingredients:

4 cups coconut milk, unsweetened (or any non-dairy milk)

1/3 cup organic sugar

1/3 cup powdered cocoa

1 teaspoon vanilla

Dash of sea salt and cinnamon

Coconut cream (opt.)

Vegan chocolate bar (opt.)

Directions:

1. Whisk all the ingredients into a 2 qt. slow cooker. Mix thoroughly. Don't worry if the cocoa powder doesn't dissolve completely.

2. Cover and cook on high for 1 ½ hours or until properly heated. Stir. Serve immediately or turn the slow cooker to warm.

3. Top hot chocolate with coconut cream and shaved vegan chocolate bar. Enjoy!

Cranberry Flavored Cider Drink

Preparation time: 10 minutes

Cooking time: 2 hours

Servings: 4

Ingredients:

8 cups (64 oz.) cranberry juice

6 cups (48 oz.) apple juice or apple cider

1 lemon, sliced

4 cinnamon sticks

1 tsp whole cloves

1 cup fresh cranberries, optional

Cheesecloth and string

Directions:

1. Pour cranberry juice and apple cider or apple juice into the slow cooker. Make sure mixture is not more than ¾ full. Add the lemon slices.

2. Set the cinnamon sticks and cloves in the cheesecloth.

4. Tie the cheesecloth with string, and then place in the slow cooker.

5. Add the fresh cranberries if desired. Cover and cook on high for 2 hours.

6. Reduce slow cooker setting to low. Serve when ready.

Slow Cooked Wassail

Preparation time: 20 minutes

Cooking time: 2 to 4 hours

Servings: 2

Ingredients:

96 oz. bottle apple cider

4 cups pineapple juice

2 lemon juice

1 orange

2 cinnamon sticks

2 pieces crystallized ginger (or ¼ cup organic sugar)

½ ground nutmeg (or 1 nutmeg)

¾ ground cloves (or whole cloves)

Directions:

1. Create holes in the orange and then dip cloves into holes in a way conducive for being sliced.

2. Pour all the ingredients into about 5 qt. slow cooker and then stir properly.

3. Cover and cook on low for 4 hours or on high for 2 hours.

4. Serve warm, and enjoy!

Nutmeg Flavored Apple Cider

Preparation time: 5 minutes

Cooking time: 2 hours

Servings: 1 Gallon

Ingredients:

1 gallon apple juice or apple cider

3 cinnamon sticks

2 pieces crystallized ginger (opt.)

1 orange, quartered into wedges

12 whole cloves

2 whole nutmegs

Cheesecloth and string

Directions:

1. Pour the apple cider into the slow cooker; make sure it's not more than ¾ full.

2. Dip cloves into orange wedges.

3. Pour the remaining ingredients into the cheesecloth and tie with strings.

4. Place in the slow cooker, cover and cook on high for 2 hours.

5. Reduce slow cooker setting to low, and serve when ready.

Vegan Caprese Pizza

Preparation time: 30 minutes

Cooking time: 2 hours

Servings: 4

Ingredients:

Pizza dough (or your preferred pizza dough)

1/3 cup olive oil (or more) (or basil pesto)

1 to 2 tomatoes, sliced

1 (16 oz.) fresh vegan mozzarella ball, sliced

Fresh basil leaves

Balsamic vinegar

Directions:

1. Roll out the pizza dough to form your desired thickness.

2. Oil the slow cooker generously.

3. Place the dough in the slow cooker, and brush on pesto or olive oil.

4. Cover and cook on high for 1 ½ to 2 hours.

5. About 15 minutes before the end of cooking time, add the sliced vegan cheese.

6. Turn off the slow cooker and let pizza cool for 10 minutes.

7. Remove the pizza carefully from the slow cooker, add the raw tomato slices, basil and sprinkle balsamic vinegar on top. Serve and enjoy!

Note: You can get several pizzas from one pizza dough depending on your desired pizza thickness and slow cooker size. This recipe produced 4 thin crust pizzas from the dough and it fitted in the slow cooker.

Pomegranate Spiced Wine

A slow cooked red wine spiced with cloves and cardamom to give you warmth during winter.

Preparation time: 10 minutes

Cooking time: 1 hour

Servings: 2

Ingredients:

½ inch piece of fresh ginger, sliced

5 whole cloves

5 whole cardamom pods

1 cup pomegranate juice (not blend)

1 cup red wine

¼ cup apple brandy

¼ cup sugar

Directions:

1. Pour ginger, cardamom pods and cloves into a small reusable muslin bag or a large tea ball.

2. Pour all the ingredients into a 1 ½ to 2 qt. slow cooker.

3. Cover and cook on high for 1 hour or until hot.

Vegan Lemon Blueberry Cake

Preparation time: 15 minutes

Cooking time: 1 hour, 10 minutes

Servings: 4

Ingredients:

Dry ingredients:

½ cup gluten-free whole-wheat flour

¼ tsp Stevia

1 tsp agave nectar or maple syrup to taste

¼ tsp baking powder

Wet ingredients:

1/3 cup unsweetened almond or coconut milk

¼ cup blueberries

1 tsp ground flaxseeds

2 tsp warm water

1 tsp olive oil (or pumpkin puree or applesauce)

½ tsp lemon zest

¼ tsp vanilla extract

¼ tsp lemon extract

Directions:

1. Grease the slow cooker with cooking spray or line with slow cooker liner or parchment paper. It will make this recipe oil-free.

2. Combine all the dry ingredients in a bowl and the wet ingredients in another bowl.

3. Pour the wet ingredient mixture into the dry mixed. Stir until well mixed.

4. Pour mixture into the slow cooker and spread evenly on the bottom.

5. Place a clean paper towel or dish towel between the slow cooker and its lid, so the condensation is absorbed.

6. Cook on high for 1 to 1 ½ hours or until the centre is solid and isn't indent when touched.

Vegan Poached Pears

Preparation time: 15 minutes

Cooking time: 2 hours

Servings: 6

Ingredients:

1 ½ cups dark brown sugar

1 tbsp grated ginger

2 tbsp olive oil or coconut oil

6 peeled Bosc pears, cored and cut in half

1 pint vegan vanilla ice cream

Directions:

1. Combine sugar, olive oil and ginger in a slow cooker.

2. Add the pears and toss gently to coat properly. Arrange the pears placing the cut-side down.

3. Cover and cook on high for 1 to 2 hours or until the pears are tender and a knife can easily be pierced into it.

4. Divide the pears and vegan ice cream among serving bowls. Sprinkle sauce on top and serve.

Vegan Baked Apples

Preparation time: 15 minutes

Cooking time: 6 hours

Servings: 6

Ingredients:

6 apples, cored

¼ cup raisins

2 tbsp maple syrup (or non-dairy sweetener)

For topping: Coconut milk

Directions:

1. Divide raisins, cinnamon and maple syrup between the cored apples.

2. Place apples in a slow cooker. Add ½ inch of water.

3. Cover and cook on low for 6 hours.

4. Serve plain or top with coconut milk. Enjoy!

Cooking tip: How to core apples: Use a paring knife or an apple corer to cut around the core. Cut about ¼ inch from the stem all the way around the apple. Do not cut about ½ inch at the bottom, and then drill out the core with the knife.

Ginger-Lemon Steamy Toddies

This is the perfect hot toddy for the winter; spiced with ginger and lemon.

Preparation time: 20 minutes

Cooking time: 4 hours

Servings: 14

Ingredients:

8 cups water

2 cups fresh lemon juice (or juice from 14 small lemons)

2 cups maple syrup

5 tbsp finely chopped crystallized ginger

1 (3-inch) piece peeled fresh ginger, sliced into ¼ inch-thick slices

¾ cup golden rum

¾ cup brandy

Lemon rind strips (optional)

Directions:

1. Pour water, lemon juice, maple syrup, crystallized ginger and fresh ginger into a 4 ½ qt. slow cooker.

2. Cover the slow cooker and cook on high for 4 hours. Remove the ginger slices and discard.

3. Add in the rum and brandy, and then stir.

4. Scoop mixture into mugs, and if desired, top with lemon rind strips. Enjoy!

END

Thank you for reading my book. If you enjoyed it, won't you please take a moment to leave me a review at your favorite retailer?

Thanks!

Samantha Keating

CPSIA information can be obtained
at www.ICGtesting.com
Printed in the USA
FSOW01n1031230218
44948FS